FLAMES OF REVIVAL

FLAMES OF REVIVAL

Igniting the Hearts of a
Nation Through Prayer

Elana Lynse

Crossway Books • Westchester, Illinois
A Division of Good News Publishers

First printing, 1989

Printed in the United States of America

Library of Congress Catalog Card Number 88-71806

ISBN 0-89107-511-9

To my sons,
Mark and Craig Swanson,
who have lovingly perservered
and cheerfully sacrificed,
being established and
rooted in Christ

Contents

Acknowledgements

There are those people who deserve special honor because without their help this book would not have taken form. I am deeply in debt to my parents, Rendel and Helen Smith, because they took one more chance on me, and rather lavishly, when reason should have clearly indicated that I was undeserving and beyond hope. I'm grateful to Lambert Dolphin for reading my earliest scratchings, for encouraging me, and for his enthusiasm throughout the project. Finally, my deepest thanks to the Crossway Books editorial staff for polishing my manuscript and bringing it to readable form.

Preface

Every true revival is preceded by its Pentecost. It is possible to have revivals without preaching, without churches, and without ministers, but without prayer a genuine revival is impossible.

(Frank Grenville Beardsley)[1]

The term *revival* has a long history in this country, but unfortunately the term presently carries some negative connotations which are at odds with its true history. In addition, for many modern Americans, there is something unusual or even criminal about prayer. Psychologists and militant secularists have been known to deride those who pray as mentally unbalanced, and this judgment often goes unquestioned. The U.S. Supreme Court has banished prayer from the public schools. If a group of such powerful people has decided that a certain activity must be forbidden, one may easily conclude, then there must be something unsavory or harmful about it. As it happens, this is about as far from the truth—and from history—as it is possible to wander.

I was not the most likely candidate to make this discovery, which came in a rather unusual way. A painful divorce left me spiritually vacant, and I attempted to fill the void with

Eastern mysticism, Yoga, meditation, spiritism, psychic phenomena, and various "touchy-feely" techniques. These I not
only adopted with enthusiasm, but became positively messian-
ic. I appointed myself a guru and taught them to others, and
even made something of a career out of it.

I soon moved on to "rebirthing," a form of "primal ther-
apy" in which one floats around in a vat of hot water while
breathing through a snorkel. The rarefied experience is sup-
posed to enable one to relive one's birth, though what good
that would do is far from certain. In any case, I soon discovered that people would willingly shell out $50 for each attempt
to duplicate the conditions of the womb.

After rebirthing, I discovered something called "Mind
Freedom"—a misnomer if there ever was one. This process did
not deliver the promised liberation, but did bring in some
money. Friends would part with $300 to spend two weekends
with me on a quest to lose their hangups and gain ultimate
truth.

Ultimate truth, however, is not found in any of this
quackery and casuistry. I finally discovered that it is found only
in the Lord Jesus Christ. My conversion to the Christian faith
was truly liberating and exhilarating.

At the time I was the leader of motivational seminars and
living a rather self-indulgent lifestyle, which found ample op-
portunities for expression on my frequent travels. But satisfying
desires, I discovered, did not bring relaxation but rather a
severe case of burnout. I was given a careful treatment plan
which involved plenty of rest, long daily walks, and a special
diet free of all stimulants. But after several weeks of this
regime I failed to get better. One day I returned from my walk
and promptly collapsed on the floor.

I actually thought I was going to die, something for
which I was not prepared. I had never had a consistent prayer

life and had no reason to believe that God would accept my prayers. But at that moment I wanted to pray. I asked, "God, is this a good day for me to die?," which could be answered with a simple and unavoidable yes or no. As it happened, God answered with an overwhelming flood of love which assured me beyond a shadow of a doubt that I would not die that day.

Not only so, but I felt His call to share that love with others. However, even as I sensed this call, I was still on the floor, immobile and helpless. I then asked God, "Will You help me?" To this day I am not sure how it happened, but I suddenly found myself standing up, my body strong and my mind alert. I had the most wonderful feeling that I was alive, but not in my own strength. As a child, I had heard the Bible verses about God breathing life into man, who then became a living soul. I sensed that He was breathing into me. I remembered verses such as . . . "just as Christ was raised from the dead through the glory of the Father, we too may live a new life" (Romans 6:4). These texts now became more than words to me. I too had been raised to new life.

Still, it took several months for me to fully recover. But I soon started telling people about Jesus and His redeeming love. I invented a course in conversational prayer called "The Talking to God Class." With God's help I finally arranged to attend a theological seminary and three years later graduated with a Master's degree.

I was excited about the visions of Christian service unfolding before me, but in spite of my newfound zeal found that doors kept closing in my face. My denomination banned women ministers, and I couldn't even find work as a church secretary. I was quite frustrated at first, but eventually concluded that God had other things for me to do. Meanwhile, my conversion had created a special sort of problem.

Instead of guiding my friends into the blind alleys of their senses or of Eastern religion, I was now telling them that God loved them. "Just give your life to Jesus," I would say, "and then you'll find peace and happiness." They weren't buying it. For many, it was precisely the same message that their parents had told them years ago, and which they had emphatically rejected. They now regarded me with suspicion and anger, believing that my present belief was only the latest sure surefire scheme for enlightenment, into which I was trying to recruit them.

I now understood how the boy who cried wolf must have felt. I finally had the right answer, but people were not disposed to believe me. I had what politicians call a credibility problem. The experience drove me to pray, to ask God to show me how His presence becomes real to people. His answer was: "pray."

With God's help, I eventually arrived at this plan: if I found a way to get others to pray, God would answer *their* prayers, enabling them to discover Him for themselves. Oddly enough, a friend who taught Yoga persuaded her clients to take a class in "Talking to God" from me. I took advantage of this rather ecumenical attitude and told these students to tell God anything that entered their minds, however nasty, negative, or embarrassing. The results were impressive.

For example, one prayed, "God, I don't think there is a God. Will You help me?" Not long afterward, he related a series of "coincidences" that convinced him that God lives.

One woman's prayer was astonishing but honest: "God, I hate You! Will You help me?" Her mother had died years before, but she still carried the anger from the experience. Now, to her delight, her bitterness began to evaporate. It was thrilling to see my friends discovering God in this way, but I did not stop here. Larger questions loomed.

What I wanted to know was this: how do *large* movements of God get started? What would it take for *thousands* of people at once to get a sense of God's presence, as opposed to a few individuals? Why could the Apostle Peter preach convincingly to multitudes in Biblical times? Conversely, why are some of today's evangelists ineffective, or even the butt of jokes?

My own prayer was similar to those of my students. "God, I don't see how the millions of people who need to know You will ever discover Your love. Will You help me?" I then felt led by the Holy Spirit to study the subject of prayer and revival. I plunged into research on the subject, and what I discovered about prayer and revival excited me beyond measure. In this book, my purpose is to share that knowledge and excitement with you.

PART ONE

The Spark

Prayer and Revival in Scripture

Introduction

Only a relatively few people discount the existence of God entirely, but many others might be described as "practical atheists." Their God lives at a great distance from human affairs, and clearly makes little difference in their own lives.

With some others, one would be hard-pressed to know that they believed in a personal God, as opposed to some sort of divine principle or force. For some, God is little more than a set of doctrines.

Many others, particularly in the Church, have theologically correct ideas about God but are impatient. They look at Biblical history and at their own situation, and wonder why God doesn't fix the world right now. They can see that God has acted, but what does it take, they ask, to get God to act at the present time?

The proper area of study to resolve this question is the Scripture. Three examples from the Old Testament show how powerful movements of God got started. And although God is the primary agent in all cases, it may surprise some to learn who made the first move.

CHAPTER ONE

How Movements of God Started

Moses in Egypt

As the book of Genesis explains, through God's providence the Hebrew people avoided famine in their own land. In Egypt, God wrought miracles through Joseph, who was acclaimed throughout the land. Joseph's people soon found themselves enjoying the good life in a foreign country. But with the passage of time, the Egyptians came to resent the prospering, proliferating Hebrews. A new king arose who knew not Joseph and who began to oppress and even exterminate Joseph's people. Then came Moses, a Hebrew raised in the royal palace by Pharaoh's daughter.

At first, Moses tried to take the plight of his people on himself and to deliver them in his own strength. When he saw an Egyptian beating a Hebrew, he killed the offender. His violent revolt, however, came to nothing, and Moses was forced to flee for his very life. The former prince who had lived in luxury and never worked wound up living in the backside of the desert and herding sheep for a living. But back in Egypt, the people were stirring in a different way:

> Years later the king of Egypt died, but the Israelites were still groaning under their slavery and cried out for help.

Their cry went up to God, who heard their groaning and remembered his covenant with Abraham, Isaac, and Jacob. He saw the slavery of the Israelites and was concerned for them. (Exodus 2:23-25, *Today's English Version*)

In short, the Israelites remembered the God of their fathers, who had brought them into Egypt in the first place. They doubtless remembered the miracles of Abraham's faith and Sarah's conception, Isaac on the altar, and Jacob's dream of a ladder reaching to Heaven. At last, they may well have prayed a prayer something like this:

O God, our God, the God of our ancestors, we need You. Hear us now and help us before we perish from the earth. We are helpless to save ourselves. Please, God, forgive us for forgetting You in our time of plenty. Forgive us, and remember us now in our distress.

Whatever the nature of their prayers, it cannot be denied that God heard them and acted. He appeared to Moses in the burning bush. He put Moses through a grueling course in spiritual leadership, which changed him from a man confident of his own powers to one who trusted in those of the Almighty. God transformed Moses from one who rashly spoke to one who humbly listened. Moses was also changed from a man characterized by hesitation to one ready to act on what God had revealed to him.

The revival of the Israelites' faith in God, and their ensuing liberation from Egypt, however, were not the work of Moses but of God. But it all began when an entire people began to pray in earnest. The Exodus establishes a pattern: prayer precedes deliverance.

Samuel in Israel

As the Scriptures abundantly note, once God's people were back in their own land, things did not always go well. Again and again they forgot the God of their fathers, went chasing after foreign gods, and fell into corruption and oppression as a result.

During one troublesome time, a woman named Hannah lived in despair. Her situation was something of a soap opera. She not only had to share her husband with another woman, but the other woman steadily produced babies, while Hannah was barren. The fruitful wife cruelly taunted Hannah, leaving her ashamed and humiliated, and finally even unable to eat.

Eventually Hannah threw herself on God's mercy and pleaded with him for a child, promising to dedicate him to the Lord. When Eli, a corrupt priest, saw her mouth moving in prayer, he thought she might be drunk. This clearly indicates how far the people had strayed from God and how vain and mechanical their worship and spiritual life had become. Apparently even the High Priest had never prayed nor seen anyone else do it. But Hannah's prayer was heard.

God honored her with a son, and she prayed in response:

> My heart rejoices in the Lord; in the Lord my horn is lifted high. My mouth boasts over my enemies, for I delight in your deliverance. There is no one holy like the Lord; there is no one besides you; there is no Rock like our God. . . . He raises the poor from the dust and lifts the needy from the ash heap; he seats them with princes and has them inherit a throne of honor. (1 Samuel 2:1, 2, 8)

This prayer later became an inspiration for that of Mary, the mother of Jesus, who, given the news of the coming Savior, prayed:

> My soul praises the Lord and my spirit rejoices in God
> my Savior, for he has been mindful of the humble state of
> his servant. . . . He has performed mighty deeds with his
> arm. (Luke 1:47, 48, 51)

While the birth of Hannah's child was not of the magnitude of Mary's, Hannah kept her vow and dedicated the child to God. Samuel became a great prophet in Israel, a precursor to the era of David, under which Israel became a great power. In the final analysis, the prayers of one brokenhearted woman, crying out in loneliness, became the spark that ignited a revival.

Nehemiah: Rebirth and Rebuilding

There arose a series of kings in Israel and Judah whose iniquities eventually led the nation into captivity in Babylon and Assyria. The return of the nation of Israel from captivity and the rebuilding of its Temple were momentous—even miraculous—events to be sure. But behind the scenes were the prayers of God's people. One may be sure that the rigors of captivity in a foreign land caused the Israelites to turn to God, just as they had in Egypt.

But things were still not well once the people were back in the land. The wall of Jerusalem had been smashed and its gates put to the torch. Nehemiah, a Jew, was cupbearer to King Artaxerxes, and in that post he learned of the disastrous situation. His distress was evident to all, and the king, with whom he clearly had a pleasant relationship, asked what was troubling him. Nehemiah explained the situation, and, doubtless to Nehemiah's surprise, the king asked him what he wanted. Immediately, he writes, "I *prayed* to the God of heaven" (Nehemiah 2:4, emphasis added).

Here was a man in constant touch with God. And his

prayer was immediately answered. Artaxerxes granted him a leave of absence, all the necessary passes and permissions, and a mandate to rebuild the wall of Jerusalem and institute certain reforms.

Nehemiah was also careful to acknowledge the mercy and power of God, and to confess the sins of the people. "Let thine ear now be attentive," he prayed,

> and thine eyes open, that thou mayest hear the prayer of thy servant, which I pray before thee now, day and night, for the children of Israel thy servants, and confess the sins of the children of Israel, which we have sinned against thee: both I and my father's house have sinned. . . . Remember, I beseech thee, the word that thou commandest thy servant Moses, saying, If ye transgress, I will scatter you abroad among the nations: but if ye turn unto me, and keep my commandments, and do them; though there were of you cast out unto the uttermost part of the heaven, yet will I gather them from thence, and will bring them unto the place that I have chosen to set my name there. (Nehemiah 1:6-9, KJV)

The final result was a new wall, a new Temple (the subject of the book of Ezra), and ultimately a new nation. Through prayer they reinstituted their traditional spiritual values and preserved their cultural heritage. That is part of what revival is all about.

CHAPTER TWO

Intercessors in Scripture

Abraham

Prayer is most poignant, most vital, when it is offered on behalf of someone else. One example of intercessory prayer is that of Abraham pleading for the city of Sodom:

> And Abraham drew near and said, Wilt thou also destroy the righteous with the wicked? Peradventure there be fifty righteous within the city: wilt thou also destroy and not spare the place for the fifty righteous that are therein? That be far from thee to do after this manner, to slay the righteous with the wicked; and that the righteous should be as the wicked, that be far from thee: Shall not the Judge of all the earth do right? And the Lord said, If I find in Sodom fifty righteous within the city, then I will spare all the place for their sakes. (Genesis 18:23-26, KJV)

This dialogue continues until God agrees not to destroy the city for the sake of *ten* righteous people out of a population likely well into the thousands. One notes that it was Abraham who ended the intercession; he seemed to be satisfied that if there were less than ten righteous, the city was deserving of any judgment God cared to bring. But one is entitled to wonder what would have happened if the partriarch had continued his pleading. Would God have spared the city for five righteous? Or two? Actually, God more than answered Abraham's prayer. The city was destroyed, but not until the God-fearing people had been safely evacuated. Lot's wife was a further casualty. She looked back and was turned into a pillar of salt.

What inspires us in this account is the sorrow of Abraham for the sins of others and his willingness to plead with God on their behalf. As in other junctures of his life, he was rewarded. He knocked, and it was opened unto him. Others benefited from his zeal.

Moses

Moses' use of prayer as a powerful conduit to God did not cease after the Israelites passed through their national baptism in the Red Sea, with Pharaoh's army in hot pursuit. At that time, his troubles were only beginning.

The people were perversely stiff-necked and often complained. As the eleventh chapter of Numbers records, Moses "prayed unto the Lord" when wrath was unleashed against the people. After the people fabricated the golden calf, Moses asked God to blot him out, if this great sin could not be forgiven. On another occasion, he prayed:

> O Lord God, destroy not thy people and thine inheritance, which thou hast redeemed through thy greatness, which thou hast brought forth out of Egypt with a mighty hand. Remember thy servants, Abraham, Isaac, and Jacob; look not unto the stubbornness of this peo-

ple, nor to their wickedness, nor to their sin: lest the land
whence thou broughtest us out say, Because the Lord
was not able to bring them into the land which he
promised them, and because he hated them, he hath
brought them out to slay them in the wilderness. Yet they
are thy people and thine inheritance, which thou
broughtest out by thy mighty power and by thy
stretched out arm. (Deuteronomy 9:26-29, KJV)

Notice Moses' trust in God's faithfulness. He clearly understood that God was far more willing and able to keep His
covenant with the people than the people were to sustain
their faith in Him. Moses did not argue on behalf of the
people's goodness, but with a view to the glory of God, the
maintenance of His holy name.

Solomon

One of the longest prayers in the Bible is Solomon's dedication
of the Temple, found in 2 Chronicles 6:14-42. Though the
occasion was ceremonial, the prayer was far from merely formal. Solomon clearly recognizes the nature of God: "But will
God really dwell on earth with men? The heavens, even the
highest heavens, cannot contain you. How much less this temple I have built."

Moreover, the prayer fairly pulses with the king's intercession for the possible (and likely) future sins of the people:
"When a man wrongs his neighbor . . . When your people
Israel have been defeated . . . When they sin against you," and
so on. The core of the prayer is a supplication repeated seven
times: "then from heaven, your dwelling place, hear their
prayer and their pleas, and uphold their cause. And forgive
your people, who have sinned against you."

It is of some significance that the one doing the praying is a king; as such he represented his people. The answer God gave to Solomon, in a dream, is one of the most quoted verses in the Bible:

> I have heard thy prayer, and have chosen this place to myself for a house of sacrifice . . . if my people, which are called by my name, shall humble themselves, and pray, and seek my face, and turn from their wicked ways, then will I hear from heaven, and will forgive their sin, and will heal their land. (2 Chronicles 7:12-14, KJV)

That was the way it happened, on more than one occasion. Solomon's own behavior, in fact, became the cause for much repentance. But God did heal the land, as He had promised. As will be seen in other sections, this type of healing is a key component of revival.

Asa and Hezekiah

In both Israel and Judah, unrighteous kings far outnumber the righteous ones. Two exceptions to the rule were Hezekiah and Asa. Hezekiah prayed for deliverance from the king of Assyria, and his prayer was in the style of Moses. "Now therefore, O Lord our God," he prayed, "I beseech thee, save thou us out of his hand, that all the kingdoms of the earth may know that thou art the Lord God, even thou only" (2 Kings 19:19, KJV).

Similarly, Asa cried to the Lord in a time of national danger. "Lord, it is nothing with thee to help," he prayed, "whether with many, or with them that have no power: help us, O Lord our God, for we rest on thee, and in thy name we go against this multitude." He added, "O Lord, thou art our God; let not man prevail against thee" (2 Chronicles 14:11, KJV).

The three kings outlined above, though far from perfect, certainly understood who the true Sovereign was. In times of trial, they sought the face of God.

Daniel

Throughout Scripture, one notes that those through whom God accomplishes the mightiest deeds are those most aware of their own shortcomings. They are also those who are willing to accept the shortcomings of their brothers and sisters as their own. At a critical point in his life, Daniel turned to God and said:

> To the Lord our God belong mercies and forgivenesses, though we have rebelled against him; neither have we obeyed the voice of the Lord our God, to walk in his laws, which he set before us by his servants the prophets. Yea, all Israel have transgressed thy law, even by departing, that they might not obey thy voice; therefore the curse is poured upon us, and the oath that is written in the law of Moses the servant of God, because we have sinned against him. . . . Now therefore, O our God, hear the prayer of thy servant, and his supplications, and cause thy face to shine upon thy sanctuary that is desolate, for the Lord's sake. O my God, incline thine ear, and hear; open thine eyes, and behold our desolations, and the city which is called by thy name; for we do not present our supplications before thee for our righteousnesses, but for thy great mercies. O Lord, hear; O Lord, forgive; O Lord, hearken and do; defer not, for thine own sake, O my God: for thy city and thy people are called by thy name. (Daniel 9:9-19, KJV)

It might be pointed out that Daniel's prayer, like that of Moses or Abraham, could have easily been accusative. But in each case, mercy triumphs over judgment. This is a prayer that should be read often, in its entirety. And it couldn't hurt to be on one's knees during the reading.

Ezra

While the rebuilding of the wall of Jerusalem fell to Nehemiah, Ezra's task concerned the Temple. Like Nehemiah, he was concerned with the spiritual condition of his people. When he learned of violations of the Law, he tore his clothes and even ripped out part of his beard. His prayer, like that of Solomon, is lengthy, but some excerpts are most worthy of quotation.

> . . . Because of our sins, we and our kings and our priests
> have been subjected to the sword and captivity, to pillage
> and humiliation. . . . What has happened is a result of our
> evil deeds and our great guilt, and yet, our God, you have
> punished us less than our sins have deserved and have
> given us a remnant like this. (Ezra 9:6-13)

It is undeniable that Ezra's fervent prayers, like those of Nehemiah, played a major role in the rebuilding of the nation.

Apostolic Intercessors

Every epistle of the Apostle Paul brims with prayer on behalf of his fellow-Christians, especially those who were in difficult circumstances. He and the other apostles also urged the offering of prayer for those in authority, that peace might prevail. Paul mentions one early Christian, Epaphras, who was "always wrestling in prayer for you" (Colossians 4:12). In the book of Revelation, we are told that the incense ascending before the throne is the prayers of the saints (Revelation 5:8).

Divine Intercession

In a sense the life, death, and resurrection of our Lord Jesus Christ, as recorded in the Gospels, reveals a life of lived-out intercessory prayer. At the very point at which He is most brutalized and vilified, He asks the Father to forgive the offenders.

Jesus' public prayers tended to be brief, which would be in keeping with His exhortations regarding the dangers of spiritual exhibitionism. But at one point we are allowed to eavesdrop as the Savior intercedes with the Father concerning those who followed Him, both at that time and in the future.

> I pray not that thou shouldest take them out of the world, but that thou shouldst keep them from the evil. They are not of the world, even as I am not of the world. Sanctify them through thy truth; thy word is truth. As thou has sent me into the world, even so have I also sent them into the world. (John 17:15-18, KJV)

Since it is the perfect, sinless Son of God making this request, it is quite impossible that it should fail to be granted. In a sense, every Christian is part of the answer.

Further, normally one doesn't think of the Holy Spirit as being an intercessor, but the Scriptures do indeed give the third member of the Trinity that role. Should we be in a situation in which we don't know how to pray, we need not be in distress. "The Spirit himself intercedes for us," Paul writes, "with groans that words cannot express." In addition, "the Spirit intercedes for the saints in accordance with God's will" (Romans 8:26, 27).

CHAPTER THREE

Principles of Revival from the Prophets

As is the case with prayers, the various prophetic proclamations in Scripture reveal important principles for revival. While a discussion of all these principles is beyond the scope of this book, the key points will be taken up.

God Never Changes

Were the God we worship a malleable, fickle being, we would have little hope for salvation, let alone revival. As the Apostle James put it, there are no "shifting shadows" with God (James 1:17). The same principle had been proclaimed long before.

Consider the prophet Habakkuk, who lived nearly 2700 years ago: "Lord, I have heard the report about Thee, and Thy work, and I fear. O Lord, revive Thy work in the midst of the years, in the midst of the years make it known; in wrath remember mercy" (Habakkuk 3:2, NASB). This is a man who dares to believe that as God has done before, so He can and will do again.

Everybody Needs God

At one rather dark point in the history of Israel, the word of the Lord came to the prophet Zechariah:

> Thus says the Lord of hosts: "It will yet be that peoples will come, even the inhabitants of many cities; and the inhabitants of one will to go another, saying, 'Let us go at once to entreat the favor of the Lord, and to seek the Lord of hosts; I will also go.' So many peoples and mighty nations will come to seek the Lord of Hosts in Jerusalem and to entreat the favor of the Lord." Thus says the Lord of hosts, "In those days ten men from the nations of every tongue will grasp the garment of a Jew, saying, 'Let us go with you, for we have heard that God is with you.'" (Zechariah 8:20-23, NASB)

One should remember that in the New Testament, "Jew" is redefined. No longer is it a strictly nationalistic or ethnic concept, or a question of circumcision. A true Jew is one who belongs to God, whose circumcision is of the heart (see Romans 2:29). In like manner, the apostles refer to the bodies of believers, individual and collective, as the temple of God (see 1 Corinthians 6:19 and 1 Peter 2:4-10).

The thrust of the prophets' message is that of a universal gospel message, in the sense that the message is directed to everyone. The Apostle Peter related a similar message, as we will see in the next section.

God Does Not Play Favorites

After the crucifixion and resurrection of Christ, on the Day of Pentecost Peter faced a multitude and quoted these words:

> And afterward, I will pour out my Spirit on all people. Your sons and daughters will prophesy, your old men will dream dreams, your young men will see visions. Even on my servants, both men and women, I will pour out my Spirit in those days. (Joel 2:28, 29)

The key phrase in the passage is *"all people."* While Scripture is clear that salvation does not go to all people without *exception*, the gospel message goes to all people and nations without *distinction*. God is not a respecter of persons, and the fact that He has worked through the nation of Israel means primarily that Israel accrues additional responsibility rather than privilege.

It should be added that no one group now monopolizes the distribution of God's spiritual gifts. The Holy Spirit gives these to the Church, as it suits Him, for the edification of the Body of Christ and the glory of God.

Jesus Christ Is Lord

The oracle of the prophet Micah included the following:

> But in the last days it shall come to pass that the mountain of the house of the Lord shall be established in the top of the mountains, and it shall be exalted above the hills; and people shall flow unto it. And many nations shall come, and say, Come, and let us go up to the mountain of the Lord, and to the house of the God of Jacob, and he will teach us of his ways, and we will walk in his paths: for the law shall go forth of Zion, and the word of the Lord from Jerusalem. And he shall judge among many people, and rebuke strong nations afar off; and they shall beat their swords into plowshares, and their spears into pruning hooks: nation shall not lift up a sword against nation, neither shall they learn war any more. (Micah 4:1-4, KJV)

Here the prophet foresees a time when knowing Jesus will be regarded as the true religion, high above all other alleged paths to God. The Lord gave Micah a vision for worldwide recognition of the one God whose standard all must obey. All nations will eventually recognize His preeminence and accept His authority. While the final manifestation of that will be in the Kingdom of God, the sovereignty and Lordship of Christ are key principles for revival in our present, troubled time.

The Need to Do Right

The prophet Isaiah stressed the importance of repentance in revival:

> . . . till the Spirit is poured upon us from on high, and the desert becomes a fertile field, and the fertile field seems like a forest. Justice will dwell in the desert and righteousness live in the fertile field. The fruit of righteousness will be peace; the effect of righteousness will be quietness and confidence forever. My people will live in peaceful dwelling places, in secure homes, in undisturbed places of rest. (Isaiah 32:15-18)

Isaiah understood that abundance, safety, and fertility on earth depended on the success of the God-man relationship. The lesson is simple: when the people of God do what is right, the result is peace, security, and freedom from stress. These are conditions that promote the healing of the Church and the land. These are the conditions that promote revival.

Summary

In the thousands of years of human history covered in the Scriptures, prayer was a vital component of life, and often led to major movements of God. It never would have occurred to those of Biblical times that prayer was something that ought to be limited by the state. Few, if any, would have thought that prayer to God was a sign of immaturity or mental imbalance.

Moderns tend to divide history into huge chunks which are sealed off from each other. Under such a system, the whole realm of Biblical history can be written off as "ancient," with the implication being that it is no longer relevant for modern times. A look at the role of prayer and revival in America's history confirms that such is not the case. To that neglected subject we now turn.

PART TWO

The Flame

Prayer and Revival in America

CHAPTER FOUR

Religious Roots

America was born in a revival of religion.
(Calvin Coolidge)

Most people learn about American history in the public schools, which is unfortunate for two reasons. First, the knowledge they gain is sketchy and often superficial. Second, public education often minimizes, ignores, or even denigrates the contributions of Christianity and religious people in general. Psychologist Paul Vitz studied school textbooks and found that they systematically avoided religious themes and people.[1] Adding to the problem is the fact that most citizens do not study the subject on their own after graduation.

Even a cursory examination suggests that it is impossible to understand American history and American democracy without full consideration of the role of Christianity and prayer. These constitute the spiritual roots of the nation, and there is no getting around that fact. Without being fanciful, it is possible to see the forces gathering long before the nation was officially founded.

Within twenty-five years after Christopher Columbus discovered America in 1492, Martin Luther nailed his Ninety-five

Theses to a church door in Wittenberg. Soon the winds of change and reformation were blowing throughout Europe, which was altered forever. One hundred years later, when the Counter-Reformation was on the rampage, Christians found safe haven in the open spaces of the New World, where there was freedom from the tyranny of state-controlled religion.

Jonathan Edwards (1703-1758) was the foremost theologian and one of the greatest minds in American history. Edwards wrote that

> This New World is probably new discovered, that the new and most glorious state of God's church on earth might commence there; that God might in it begin a new world in a spiritual respect, when he creates the new heavens and the new earth.[2]

The religious motivations of the settlers, however, did not guarantee that all would be perfect or even tranquil in the new land. Some of the groups, having escaped religious tyranny, proceeded to impose it on the other Christians. And some of the settlers came for motives other than religious freedom. There were fortunes to be made.

Nonetheless, the history of the United States resembles that of ancient Israel on a number of points. Not that the United States is "chosen" in the same sense Israel was, even though some of the settlers aimed to create a "city set on a hill." The role of Israel in that regard was unique. But Americans have had to deal with the same kinds of problems: corruption, immorality, war, and sinfulness in general. But as in ancient Israel, there were seasons of revival, both in American churches and in the society at large.

A number of scholarly works have been written on this subject, and this book will not attempt to duplicate them. Part of my purpose is to get readers to study this vast but neglected material (see Bibliography) for themselves. These scholarly works, however, do not always trace revival from the point at which it actually begins. An erroneous impression is that revivals were the work of outstanding, charismatic individuals. While that is partly true, the prominent individuals were seldom the first step.

Cycles of Prayer

Table I outlines the great movements of prayer in American history. It shows that prominent revivals and awakenings were begun and sustained by the cries of our people in prayer. It confirms that, with brief periods of interruption, prayer has bathed our country for two hundred years.

The Moravian Prayer Vigil actually started in Europe in 1727 and promoted prayer for the worldwide advancement of Christianity. This vigil lasted one hundred years and actually overlapped the Concert of Prayer, which will be taken up later. Its origins are of considerable interest.

When the cadres of the Counter-Reformation were persecuting Moravians and other followers of Martin Luther, Count Nikolaus Ludwig von Zinzendorf (1700-1760) offered them sanctuary on his estates. With Zinzendorf, the believers were safe, but other problems arose. Theological disputes threatened the harmony between these groups. And as is often the case, the disputes centered not on the great doctrines of the faith, but on petty details of religious practice. The bickering reached such a fervor that something had to be done if the groups were to carry on together and not destroy themselves. They arrived at a simple answer: prayer. Changing the focus to God is a good way to get people's eyes off each other.

All agreed to join hearts in prayer and to bind their differences in love. These meetings for prayer began in Ger-

47

TABLE I
CYCLES OF PRAYER

YEAR	PRAYER CYCLE	RESULTING LEADERS, PREACHERS, EXPANSION
1727	Moravian Prayer Vigil (duration: 100 years)	1727 Frelinghuysen, New Jersey; 1734 Jonathan Edwards; 1739 Wesley, Whitefield
1792	Concert of Prayer (duration: 50 years)	1800s frontier revival, formation of missionary societies, Charles Finney; 1840 Y.M.C.A., the great nineteenth century of expansion
1858	The Noon Prayer Hour (duration: 25 years)	C. H. Spurgeon, Salvation Army; 1873 D. L. Moody, China Inland Mission, Y.M.C.As flourish; era of lay ministry expansion
1905	"Year of the Holy Spirit" (duration: until WWI)	Worldwide awakening; birth of Pentecostal denominations
1914 on	Decades dominated by rally evangelism. Tabernacle evangelists. Billy Sunday. 1950s—Eisenhower Awakening, Billy Graham. 1960s counter-revival. 1970s Jesus Movement.	

many on May 12, 1727. Having apparently solved the problems of schism and disunity, the believers went on to cover matters greater than any petty doctrinal dispute. The Moravians prayed fervently for a great outpouring of God's Holy Spirit throughout the entire world. The various groups carried on these prayers constantly for one hundred years. And the revival that followed in their wake lasted nearly two centuries.

Prayer Revival Spreads West

Theodore Frelinghuysen came to the Raritan Valley of New Jersey in the Fall of 1727. He had been trained by the Moravians and was a man of fervent prayer whose preaching carried great power. His method was to select lay leaders and teach them how to conduct prayer and Bible study meetings in their homes.

This kind of tactic was not the normal practice at the time, and some church leaders attacked Frelinghuysen.[3] These attacks inspired Jonathan Edwards to write a response under the title "A Thousand Imprudences Will Not Prove a Work to Be Not of the Spirit of God." His remarks indicate the pervasive influence and spiritual power of this early prayer awakening:

> It is not reasonable to determine that a work is not from God's Holy Spirit because of the extraordinary degree in which the minds of persons are influenced. If they seem to have an extraordinary conviction of the dreadful nature of sin, and a very uncommon sense of the misery of a Christless condition—or extraordinary views of the certainty and glory of divine things—and are proportionably moved with very extraordinary affections of fear and sorrow, desire, love, or joy; or if the apparent change be very sudden, and the work be carried on with very unusual swiftness—and the persons affected are very numerous, and many of them are very young, without unusual circumstances, not infringing upon Scripture marks of a work of the Spirit—these things are no argument that the work is not of the Spirit of God.[4]

John Wesley's ministry of prayer and teaching had also been influenced by the Moravians, who were still holding their prayer meetings in Germany. Wesley's "societies" were lay-led groups that met weekly in homes for prayer, Bible study, and confession of faults. Benjamin Franklin testified to the widespread popularity of these neighborhood meetings for prayer in his autobiography in 1739. He wrote that "it seemed as if all the world were growing religious so that one could not walk through the town on an evening without hearing psalms sung by different families of every street."[5]

Jonathan Edwards also noted the progress of this awakening, as he had that of Frelinghuysen. He wrote:

> There has formerly sometimes been a remarkable awakening and success of the means of grace in some particular congregation, and this used to be much taken notice of and acknowledged to be glorious, though the towns and congregations round continued dead. But now God has brought to pass a new thing: He has wrought a great work of this nature, that has extended from one end of the land to the other.[6]

This was true. By 1739 the prayer revival had reached most American families. It would later affect the way American government would be established.

The generation that drafted the Constitution and established American government grew to maturity under the powerful influences of prayer and piety. And piety, it should be stressed, did not have the superficial, negative connotation it does today. It involved a true spirituality and was quite public-spirited.[7] In those days, the neighborhood prayer meeting was an institution and became the model for a decision by vote. This was a radical development at the time.

It should be remembered that the European political model was the divine right of kings, the idea that the monarch received his authority for rule directly from God, and that it was the divine duty of everyone else to do precisely as he said. In religious circles, there was a special priestly class—as in Roman Catholicism—mediating between men and God. And in many Protestant state churches, the clerics upheld the divine right of kings and generally promoted a two-tiered society: kings, priests, and religious dignitaries, with many special privileges, on one hand; and the common herd, without similar rights, on the other. It was a fundamentally unjust setup that the Reformation and lay-led prayer movements helped to change.

A key teaching of the Reformation was the priesthood of the believer. This doctrine disavowed the need for a special priestly class to mediate between men and God. As the Scriptures clearly taught, all Christians were indwelt by the Holy Spirit and had access to God through the one mediator between men and God, Jesus Christ, who functions as the believer's sole High Priest. Indeed, He is uniquely equipped to do so, since He shares in their humanity and was tempted in all ways as they were, but without sin.

This doctrine formed the basis for the lay-led prayer meeting, in which *all* participated. This had an egalitarian effect and formed a model for decision by vote. As historian William Warren Sweet has noted: "Revivals were a great leveling force in American colonial society; they sowed the basic seeds of democracy more widely than any other single influence."[8]

In every neighborhood, on every block, children, grandparents, fathers, mothers, rich, and poor joined in singing, praise, and prayer. At home, women had leadership authority and could lead prayer, teach, and counsel. At first, prominent figures such as Wesley chose the group leaders, but the groups themselves eventually took over this function. In this process lies the seeds of the neighborhood or precinct representation so vital to the democratic process.

Neighborhood prayer meetings were particularly strong among the various Baptist groups. Historian W. L. Muncy, Jr. has observed:

As the period of the American Revolution approached, the political leaders of Virginia and the other colonies found that their ideas of political freedom and democracy were akin to the ideas of these Baptists concerning religious freedom and church polity. This gave the Baptists an influence among leaders of life and thought which they did not possess before. The course of events which brought about the Revolution and the independence of the thirteen colonies made it possible for the Baptists to grow in influence as well as in numbers.[9]

The non-hierarchical form of church government established by the Puritans was another basis for American democracy. As William Warren Sweet observed: "American democracy owes much to Puritanism. . . . . In adopting the congregational form of church polity in New England, Puritans planted the seed of pure democracy in American soil."[10]

These reforms were not without costs or opposition. Conflicts with the Old World were inevitable. While Christians of the time were divided over the merits of the the War of Independence, it is hard to deny that the conflict enabled the colonies to make a clean break, a fresh start.

At the beginning of that war, Congress formally expressed its desire "to have all the people of all ranks and degrees duly impressed with a solemn sense of God's superintending providence, and of their duty to rely in all their lawful enterprises on his aid and direction." Leaders proclaimed a fast, so that the people might confess their sins, repent, and pray, and "through the merits of Jesus Christ obtain forgiveness." While the war still raged, General George Washington issued an order commanding proper respect for the Sabbath by the troops.

Not all the Founding Fathers were Christians, but most

had a reverence for God and God's order of things. They recognized the vital link between religious life and the nation's formation. Consider the words of Benjamin Franklin at age eighty. The passage is lengthy, but worthy of quotation in full:

> In this situation of this assembly, groping, as it were, in the dark to find political truth, and scarce able to distinguish it when presented to us, how has it happened, Sir, that we have not hitherto once thought of humbly applying to the Father of Lights to illuminate our understandings? In the beginning of the contest with Great Britain, when we were sensible of danger, we had daily prayer in this room for divine protection. Our prayers, Sir, were heard and they were graciously answered. All of us who were engaged in the struggle must have observed the frequent instances of a superintending providence in our favor. To that kind providence, we own this happy opportunity of consulting in peace on the means of establishing our future national felicity. And have we now forgotten this powerful friend? Or do we imagine that we no longer need His assistance? I have lived, Sir, a long time and the longer I live, the more convincing proofs I see of this truth, that God governs in the affairs of men. And if a sparrow cannot fall to the ground without His notice, is it possible that an empire can rise without His aid? We have been assured, Sir, in the Sacred Writings, that "except the Lord build the house, they labor in vain that built it." I firmly believe this: and I also believe that without his concurring aid, we shall succeed in this political building no better than the builders of Babel; we shall be divided by our little, partial local interests, our prospects will be confounded and we ourselves shall become a reproach and a by-word down to future ages. And, what is worse, mankind may hereafter, from this unfortunate instance, despair of establishing government by hu-

man wisdom, and leave it to chance, war, and conquest.

I therefore beg leave to move, that henceforth prayers, imploring the assistance of Heaven and its blessing on our deliberations, be held in this assembly every morning before we proceed to business, and that one or more of the clergy of this city be requested to officiate in that service.[11]

It should be added that Franklin never made a clear profession of Christian faith; yet his vision of God's power, and its role in the formation of the country, is abundantly clear.

Franklin and other founders knew that the state-run churches of Europe punished those who would not conform to their doctrines and practices. It was for this reason that the early Americans forbade the government to establish an official church, and to hinder the free exercise of religion. The phrase "separation of church and state" nowhere appears in the Constitution. There is only an "establishment clause" and a "free exercise" clause, with the former in service of the latter.

The lack of an official church most emphatically did not mean that politics and education were to be kept beyond the reach of religious values. The Framers knew full well that religion was vital to both. The notion that prayer, formal or otherwise, ought to be banished from the schools would have been repugnant to them. Indeed, many of our most prestigious universities—Brown, Columbia, Dartmouth, Princeton, Rutgers—began as seminaries, and were a direct result of religious revival. The government could also help religious groups, as long as it did not show favoritism.

One of the great blots on the record of the New World was slavery. Democracy is a sham if some women and men are the property of others. But slavery, it should be stressed, did not distinguish the New World from a thousand other societies, including many in Africa itself. It was the efforts to *abolish* slavery that were unprecedented. And if strict "separation of church and state" had been in effect, the brutal trade might still be in effect.

Contrary to what is often currently taught, even at the university level, it was the *religious awakening* that launched the attack on slavery. The Biblical idea that all people were created in the image of God, and were therefore of infinite value to Him, was clearly inconsistent with slavery. On that basis, prominent evangelical preachers such as George Whitefield not only attacked the institution of slavery on a Biblical basis, but established schools for blacks. It is also seldom recognized that Rev. Martin Luther King, Jr.'s efforts against segregation and Jim Crow laws were religiously motivated. A strict "separation" view would have declared much of the civil rights movement an illegitimate intrusion of religion into public life.

In summary, the brotherhood and harmony of the prayer movement in the New World tended to erode social class distinctions and enhance the value of the individual before God and in government. This paved the way for voting and for the abolition of forced servitude. The neighborhood prayer meetings were schools of leadership, the source of local, grass-roots political organization and representative government, which contrasted with the system of appointments from some central authority. By recognizing the True Sovereign, they also reinforced the idea of accountability before God and one's fellows. The acknowledgment of man's sinful condition, based on familiarity with the Scriptures, led to a system of checks and balances designed to prevent some group or individual from undue domination over others. The congregational form of church government resulted in a system without rigid class distinctions. Knowledge of past repressions against Baptists and other groups by state-run churches led to a renunciation of state religion and a system of full religious freedom. As Benjamin Lacy stated, it was the Great Awakening that furnished the "dynamic power" enabling all this to take place.[12]

There were, of course, other contributions to American democracy and American life in general, and, in a diverse and pluralistic society, one must be careful with concepts such as the "Christian nation." However, the present tendency of a highly biased and secularized educational system, as well as hostile groups such as the American Civil Liberties Union, is to discount the undeniable Christian contribution to American government and society. As noted, most public school textbooks for young people make no mention of religion at all.

The Scriptures tell us that the Kingdom of God is not of this world. While far from perfect, when compared with other systems—including some such as communism which claim to be perfect—rule by, for, and of the people comes about as close to a piece of Heaven on earth as can be realized. Just ask any defector or refugee from a totalitarian state who has risked everything to gain freedom. This freedom, so prized by those who are new to it, and so neglected by those who are used to it, is part of the legacy of prayer surrounding this nation's beginnings.

CHAPTER FIVE

The Prayer Century

Christians were very much humbled . . . even impenitent men saw and felt that this was holy ground. They felt that it was awful to trifle with the place of prayer; sacrilegious to doubt the spirit, the sincerity, the efficiency or the power of prayer. . . . The Christians prayed in bold confidence. They believed that if they united to pray for any particular man's conversion, that man was sure to be converted. . . . The impact of believing prayer seemed irresistible.

(From *The Power of Prayer*, 1859)[1]

As Benjamin Franklin knew all too well, every generation faces the danger of allowing the fire of faith to flicker. This is especially true in times of relative security, peace, and prosperity. But following the pattern of the prophets in the Old Testament, the warnings of Franklin and many others went unheeded. After the War of Independence, the people relaxed their prayer vigil, allowing the nation to fall into a period of lawlessness. And there were other contributions to that period of decline and spiritual bankruptcy.

Benjamin Lacy cites five: 1) The aftermath of war, which brought about a hardness of soul in the people; 2) a period of migration, which broke up families; 3) a spirit of greed, which led to speculation and bloodshed; 4) a shortage of missionaries and evangelists in the new land; 5) the influence of the French Revolution and French Deism.[2] Deism conceived of God as a kind of celestial watchmaker who wound up His creation, then more or less abandoned it.

If the Reformation had been a spiritual revolution, these were times of secular counterrevolution. François Marie Arouet, usually known as Voltaire (1694-1778), predicted the demise of Christianity within thirty years. And as J. Kenneth Latourette has noted, it did indeed seem as though Christianity was about to be ushered out of the affairs of men.

But such a thing was not to be. God's people again began to pray in earnest. Interestingly, the movement that was to affect North America in such a powerful way again got its start in Europe.

The Concert of Prayer

The beginnings of this movement were simple enough. In 1784 a short tract was published in England calling for an outpouring of God's Holy Spirit, church unity, and prayer for the worldwide advancement of God's Kingdom. One denomination after another dedicated the first Monday of the month to pray for revival. Shortly thereafter, twenty-three ministers of New England churches issued a circular letter nearly identical to the one which had called England to prayer:

> To the ministers of and churches of every Christian denomination in the United States, to unite in their endeavors to carry into execution the humble attempt to promote explicit agreement and visible union of God's people in extraordinary prayer for the revival of religion

and the advancement of Christ's kingdom on Earth. All are invited to maintain public prayer and praise, and instruction from God's word.[3]

Regular prayer meetings for an outpouring of the Holy Spirit and outreach to the world began in those twenty-three New England churches. The first Tuesday of January 1795, and the first Tuesday of each quarter thereafter, were given to public prayer, "until the Almighty answered with a general awakening." The Concert of Prayer quickly spread throughout New England. All of the New England states, towns, and denominations were affected. Soon the prayer revival spread to the southern states and to the frontiers, filling churches and open spaces with prayer, praise, and worship. E. D. Griffin, a pastor in New Salem in the early 1800s, commented on the changes brought by the Concert of Prayer:

> The year 1792, it has often been said, ushered in a new era into the world. In that year commenced a series of revivals in America which has never been interrupted.[4]

Generally speaking, the various meetings were orderly, solemn, and devoid of emotional display. However, in meetings on the frontier, trembling, shaking, weeping, and even shouting were regular occurrences. Frequently worshipers would fall as if struck by lightning. These were eager for counsel and gladly confessed Christ. They were expressive, rejoicing with abandon, and later became earnest and faithful members.

At one open field gathering, scoffers came waving their whiskey bottles. One of the scoffers collapsed to the ground and couldn't get up. A minister came and urged him to pray for salvation, but he replied, "I'll be damned if I do." He lay there helplessly for hours and finally crept away on all fours like an animal.[5]

Overall, the results of the Concert of Prayer were remarkable. Within a few years, the post-war decline of Christianity had been turned completely around. As Edwin Orr has noted:

> Skepticism and infidelity of which there was plenty in post-revolutionary days were swept away; taverns were deserted by their erstwhile patrons; differences and prejudices were healed and brotherly love was restored, while family feuds were settled and family religion restored.[6]

A letter of one George A. Baxter, written as he journeyed through Kentucky in 1800, captures the mood of the times:

> On my way, I was informed by settlers of the road that the character of Kentucky was entirely changed and that they were as remarkable for sobriety as they had formerly been for dissoluteness and immorality. And indeed, I found Kentucky to appearances the most moral place I had ever seen. A profane expression was hardly ever heard. A religious awe seemed to pervade the country. Upon the whole, I think that the revival in Kentucky was the most extraordinary that has ever visited the church of Christ.[7]

The effects of the Concert of Prayer extended over half a century, and spread to other countries as well. As a result, Christians drew together in brotherhood, social ills were healed, and a zeal for foreign missions developed. The revival continued as long as people persisted in prayer. There was a gap of barely sixteen years before the next period of revival.

The Noon Prayer Hour

The 1850s were prosperous times in America. People were making and saving money; it was normal to find interest rates of 18 percent. But economic prosperity did not mean spiritual health for the churches, which were losing members at the time. In addition, the issue of slavery had bitterly divided both the country and the churches. The climate was one of spiritual stagnation.

It was also at this time that prophetic-minded preachers such as William Miller began preaching about the Second Coming of Jesus Christ. Unfortunately, some wild speculations surrounded this movement. Miller made the unfortunate mistake of predicting 1844 as the precise year for the Apocalypse, which led to disillusionment and humiliation for his followers when the predicted event did not occur. But all was not bleak for the nation at large. The souls of the people were stirring.

It is often difficult to pinpoint the steps that lead a people out of spiritual darkness. With Moses, the burning bush was clearly a major event, but others are not quite as clear. A small incident in Lexington may have sparked another wave of revival.

In 1856, a certain Pastor White of Lexington was told that some women had been gathering to pray for revival. Soon after, a Mr. Booker, who attended a nearby college, was accidentally shot by his close friend and roommate. He lived for two days after the accident and gave a testimony of Christ that was so earnest and urgent that many of his friends and those attending him were inspired and awakened. At one Lord's Supper service, some fify-five college students gave themselves to Christ.[8] Thus, it is entirely possible that the revival of 1858 began with a handful of women dedicating themselves to prayer. But it was not only in small towns where an awakening was taking place. Major urban areas such as New York were also affected.

In 1857, the Old Dutch Church at Fulton and William St. in Manhattan hired one Jeremiah Lanphier as a "lay visitor" to

61

reach the unchurched masses in the city. Lanphier visited every family, presenting a folder introducing himself and describing his church and its services. He paid special attention to immigrant families, who at first greeted him with suspicion or apathy.

Lanphier then conceived the idea of a noon-hour prayer meeting for the thousands of businessmen who jostled in the crowded streets. He invited them to an upstairs room at the church with a handbill written as follows:

> How often shall I pray? As often as the language of prayer is in my heart. As often as I see my need of help. As often as I feel the power of temptation. As often as I am made sensible of any spiritual declension or feel the aggression of a worldly earthly spirit. . . .
>
> A day prayer meeting is held every Wednesday from 12-1 o'clock. . . . This meeting is intended to give merchants, mechanics, clerks, strangers, and business men generally an opportunity to stop and call upon God amid the perplexities incident to their respective avocations. It will continue for one hour; but it is also designed for those who may find it inconvenient to remain more than nine or ten minutes, as well as for those who can spare the whole hour. The necessary interruption will be slight because anticipated; and those who are in haste can often expedite their business engagements by halting to lift up their voices to the throne of grace in humble, grateful prayer.
>
> All are cordially invited to attend.[9]

The first meeting was held in mid-September, 1847. Lanphier arrived ten minutes early. The clock struck 12, but no one else showed up. Lanphier, however, was not discouraged; he waited and prayed alone. At 12:35 five people came. They prayed together until the hour was up. The next week, fourteen arrived, and the week after that twenty-three. The group then began to meet daily, with attendance growing to roughly one hundred persons.

This explosion of prayer was heard all over the country, where laymen began noon prayer services in churches, stores, and public halls following Lanphier's pattern.

The following is a description of a prayer meeting in Philadelphia, typical of similar gatherings everywhere because a bill of direction was issued to all prayer leaders.

> There was no noise, no confusion. A layman conducts the meeting. Any suitable person may pray or speak to the audience for five minutes only. If he does not bring his prayer to a close in that time, a bell is touched and he gives way. One or two verses of the most spiritual hymns go up, like the sound of many waters; requests for prayer for individuals are then made, one layman or minister succeeds another in perfect order and quiet, and after a space which seems a few minutes—so strange, so absorbing, so interesting is the scene—the leader announces that it is one o'clock and, punctual to the moment a minister pronounces the benediction and the immense audience slowly, quietly and in perfect order, pass from the hall! Some ministers remain to converse in a small room off the platform with any who desire spiritual instruction.[10]

The lay leaders who presided over the meetings were chosen from every evangelical denomination. The opening, which consisted of two stanzas of a hymn, a passage of Scripture, and a prayer, was limited to ten minutes, after which the leader would announce that the meeting was open for prayer, that everyone was welcome to take part, and that everyone was to obey the rules.

There were several large signs posted in the room. One said, "No Controversial Subjects Discussed." Biblical prophecy was quite likely one of these, and baptism might have been another. A second sign urged all to obey the five minute rule. When someone would stray from prayer and begin preaching, the leaders were instructed to gently and firmly guide them back to prayer. Participants reportedly preferred meetings which had as few preliminaries as possible. They had come to pray, and pray they did.

The awakening of which they were part affected the whole nation, every city and town, schools and colleges, touching all classes of people. Religious and secular observers alike were unanimously approving, with scarcely a critical voice raised anywhere. It seemed to many that the fruits of Pentecost were being reaped a thousandfold—and that without any fanaticism. The number of reported conversions soon reached fifty thousand, and church records show an average of ten additional members per week for a period of two years.[11]

By early Spring of 1858, there were more than twenty different prayer meetings in New York City alone. In one hour, over six thousand individuals were counted at prayer in the financial district. Fire and police departments opened their doors for prayer services, as did merchants and even theatres. In fact, the directors of Burton's Theatre, at the center of New York City's commercial district, made the facility available for preaching services.

Such developments could hardly pass unnoticed. Revival was headline news, and reporters were sent to meetings. Indeed, interest was such that some of the larger New York dailies issued extra editions.[12]

Soon practically all churches were open every night. Not only so, they were packed to the rafters. People seeking prayer and religious instruction inundated every group—Protestants,

Catholics, even Unitarians. Ninety-six thousand people were reported converted to God in a few months time.[13] And the tidal wave of awakening quickly swept on.

This was not a revival that had much for the heart but nothing for the mind. In March 1858 prayer and revival swept Harvard University. Five thousand people gathered for prayer in the Academy of Music hall in Washington, D.C. In Chicago, two thousand people crowded into the Metropolitan Theatre for prayer daily, and there was a flood of revival in that city.

Churches were packed for services at 7:00 A.M., and noon and 6:30 P.M. also, daily. A Chicago Lutheran Church reporting 121 members in 1856 grew to 1400 by 1860. On the Ohio and Mississippi Rivers, people gathered for prayer on ships. Even saloons became sites for prayer meetings.

As a result of letters from Christians in the East, the revival spread to San Francisco. Churches in that city were also packed for prayer at noon and in the evenings. Mass conversions were reported. In short, practically every congregation was touched. Reports and newsletters give the flavor of the times.

In one case, a merchant from Albany arrived to purchase goods from a New York City merchant. At noon, the New Yorker asked to be excused to attend a prayer meeting. The man from Albany preferred to close the deal, as he was in a hurry. "Can't you pray enough at morning and night?" he asked. The New Yorker responded that he considered the prayer meeting more important that the sale of his entire stock of goods. He persuaded the gentleman from Albany to come with him. He went, was converted, and soon started noon prayer meetings in his own city.[14]

In a meeting in Boston, a gentleman rose and said that he had come from Omaha, Nebraska and found prayer taking place all along the route. His passage had been, in effect, a

two-thousand-mile prayer meeting.[15] A letter from Chicago
dated March 21, 1858 stated:

> The religious interest now existing in this city is very
> remarkable. More than two thousand businessmen meet
> at the noon prayer meeting. The Metropolitan Hall is
> crowded to suffocation. The interest in the First Baptist
> Church is beyond anything I have ever seen in my life.
> Some who have come to the city on business have be-
> come so distressed about their condition as sinners before
> God, that they have entirely forgotten their business in
> the earnestness of their desire for salvation. I am amazed
> to see such evidences of God's grace and power manifest-
> ed among men. I might add that the First Baptist Church
> has daily meetings from eight to nine in the morning,
> twelve to one, and at six and one half o'clock evening.
> The church today had an all-day meeting.[16]

The *Chicago Daily Press* of March 13, 1858, contained
this report on the impact of the awakening:

> A large class of our readers, we are assured, will be
> interested in such details as we have been able to collect
> in a form meeting our purpose, to the extent to which
> Chicago has shared in the general religious awakening
> that has been one of the most marked events of the year
> throughout the entire country, East and West.
>
> In the larger cities of the East and in New York
> City especially, this movement, in the increased zeal of
> Christians and the awakening and conversion of those
> previously unconcerned and careless in religious matters,
> has become a prominent topic among the news of the
> day, so large a portion of those communities have been
> sharing in and yielding to the influences at work which
> has had steady, silent and solemn progress, without noise
> or excitement.

At one large, crowded prayer meeting, a man was praying when his neighbor gave him a sharp shove with his elbow, grabbed his arm, and said, "Stop praying and tell me how I can become a Christian."

The church leaders of Kalamazoo, Michigan, launched an ecumenical prayer meeting with great trepidation. Episcopalians, Baptists, Methodists, Presbyterians, and Congregationalists had high hopes—but would the public attend? Surprisingly, the first meeting was packed. Doctrinal and ecclesiastical differences had inhibited no one.

To maintain order, the leader asked people to write their requests on slips of paper and pass them to the front where they would be read aloud. The first note read, "Please pray for my husband's conversion. He is far from God and needs our prayers." A lawyer then stood up and announced that the note must have been written by his wife, that he was far from God, that the people should pray for his conversion. Then a blacksmith arose and said that the note was written by his wife and that he needed to be converted. As the account has it, five husbands were converted in five minutes, and before long five hundred were converted in the town.[17]

Reverend John Girardeau of the Anson Street Presbyterian Church of Charleston, South Carolina, began a prayer meeting that constantly increased until the church was full. He declined to preach, however, until there was an outpouring of the Holy Spirit, for which he prayed long and hard. One evening, while he led the people in prayer, "he received a sensation as if a bolt of electricity had struck his head and diffused itself through his whole body." He said to his congregation: "The Holy Spirit has come. We will begin preaching tomorrow evening," and dismissed them. But no one left. They all began to sob quietly and remained until after midnight. The meetings continued every night for eight weeks.[18]

Revivalist preacher Charles Finney noted that the people seemed to prefer meetings for prayer over those for preaching, and that the answers to prayer had drawn national attention. Finney wrote that "the windows of Heaven were opened and the Spirit of God poured out like a flood." He also took note of special editions of the *New York Tribune*, which covered the revival across the country.[19]

A volume published in New York in 1859 noted that:

Christians pray in bold confidence. Christians were very much humbled . . . even impenitent men saw and felt that this was holy ground. They felt that it was awful to trifle with the place of prayer; sacrilegious to doubt the spirit, the sincerity, the efficiency or the power of prayer . . . that if they united to pray for any particular man's conversion, that man was sure to be converted . . . because he had become the subject of prayer. . . . The impact of believing prayer seemed irresistible. The instances given regarding the efficacy of prayer at Fulton Street were multiplied throughout the country and the people wondered.[20]

The effects were soon to spread beyond the country. Charles Spurgeon, known as the prince of preachers, was also inspired by the revival of 1858. Also as a result of that awakening, Hudson Taylor launched the China Inland Mission. Revival spread to Australia and to Africa, where Christian influence had not been strong.

When news of the revival in the United States reached Capetown, South Africa, local ministers convened a conference. Surprisingly 374 Christian leaders arrived, and all prayed together for an outpouring of God's Spirit in Africa. Fifty days later at a youth camp, during the testimony of a black girl,

There was a sound like an approaching tornado. All the youth at once rose to their feet and began to pray. When the minister in charge of the camp asked his youth director for an explanation of this strange behavior of the youth, the answer was, "It's the presence of God." The minister replied, "I hold you responsible." Nevertheless, prayer meetings multiplied in Africa.[21]

Back in America, civil war loomed. But amidst the turmoil, bloodshed, and tragedy of that conflict, God's Spirit continued to work. Thousands of Christian volunteers brought the gospel to southern soldiers. The United States Christian Association, a national agency of the newly organized Young Men's Christian Association, sent five thousand young men and women to labor among the troops.

One of those who began his ministry that way was a young man named Dwight L. Moody. Thirty years later he would write that he still met men who were converted during the Army meetings.[22] Well over a hundred years later, Moody's legacy lives on. And Moody was far from alone. Thirteen hundred ministers and other professional clergy volunteered to serve as chaplains. Some reports indicate that 150,000 men were converted during the war.

Confederate literature of the time indicated that a sense of prayer prevailed in the camps, and that roughly one third of the soldiers were men of prayer. To be sure, it is not difficult to pray in times of peril. The Confederates may have been driven to God in the awareness that they faced a superior armed force, or that their individual deaths were imminent. But reports of the time indicate that there was much more to it than simple self-preservation.

For example, the *Richmond Christian Advocate* stated that for years there had not been a revival comparable to the one then taking place in the Army. Diaries, letters, and news articles attest to the prevalence of prayer. Chaplains reported that "in place of the oath, coarse jests, and impure song so common to army camps—prayers and praises and songs of Zion were heard."[23]

One letter from the front was full of excitement about preachers who had visited camp, hardly the sort of thing one expects from a fighting man. The note stated that "a stranger would have to conclude that the Army was very religious as there were log churches every six or eight hundred yards, with prayer meetings twice a week." He went on to name some ten prominent preachers, including two generals.[24]

This was Abraham Lincoln's prayer for a nation at war:

> Grant O, merciful God, that with malice toward none, with charity to all, with firmness in the right as thou givest us to see the right, we may strive to finish the work we are in; to bind up the nation's wounds; to care for him who shall have borne the battle and for his widow and his orphan; to do all which may achieve and cherish a just and lasting peace among ourselves and with all nations.[25]

On another occasion, in 1863, Lincoln proclaimed a national fast. He noted the "supreme authority and just government of Almighty God, in all the affairs of men and of nations." The purpose of the fast was to recognize dependence on God, and to get men to

> confess their sins and transgressions, in humble sorrow, yet with assured hope that genuine repentance will lead to mercy and pardon; and to recognize the sublime truth, announced in the Holy Scriptures and proven by all history, that those nations only are blessed whose God is the Lord. . . .
> All this being done in sincerity and truth, let us

then rest humbly in the hope authorized by the Divine teachings, that the united cry of the Nation will be heard on high, and answered with blessings, no less than the pardon of our national sins, and the restoration of our now divided and suffering Country, to its former happy condition of unity and peace.[26]

Lincoln was not an especially devout man by the standards of the day. However, he knew where to direct the attention of the American people—to Almighty God—and did so without the slightest reluctance. This shows how thoroughly a spirit of prayer and revival had permeated our society in the century of prayer.

CHAPTER SIX

Onward to the Year of the Holy Spirit

Let no man suppose that progress can be divorced from religion, or that there is any platform for the ministers of reform than the platform written in the utterances of our Lord and Savior.

America was born a Christian nation. America was born to exemplify that devotion to the elements of righteousness which are derived from the revelations of the Holy Scripture. I ask of every man and woman . . . that they will realize that part of the destiny of America lies in their perusal of this great book of revelations—that if they would see America free and pure they will make their own spirits free and pure by this baptism of the Holy Scripture.

(Woodrow Wilson, 1911)[1]

If 1858 and the years that followed were movements of prayer and waiting on the Holy Spirit, as at Pentecost, then the years following 1882 were missionary years, like the work of the apostles in the book of Acts. (That book is sometimes called the "Acts of the Holy Spirit.") Twenty years of outreach followed twenty years of revival, culminating in what church historian Latourette called the "great century."

73

Lay ministry continued to surge as grass-roots interdenominational prayer for awakening proliferated throughout the 1880s. The closing years of the nineteenth century saw record strides in domestic and foreign missions as God called the youth corps of the war years to service in other fields. Christ's Kingdom steadily expanded, culminating in a worldwide revival in 1904. One of its centers was in Wales, in the British Isles.

Welsh miners were hard, somber types, normally unmoved by spiritual matters. However, the prayers of God's people again touched off revival. They started in prayer groups of less than twenty, and within two years all the churches in Wales were filled each evening. Some churches were packed from 6:00 A.M. until after midnight. One hundred thousand conversions were reported in a two-year period, and those converted were still leading vigorous Christian lives in the 1930s.

Evan Roberts, a leading figure of the awakening, insisted that prayer was more important than his preaching. To prove it, he would not announce where he was going to preach on any given night. No one knew just where he would show up.

Several thousand gathered at one church to pray, and Roberts stood up in their midst. He asked, "How many believe in the promises of God?" and hearty amens were heard all around. "Would you agree that a promise made by Jesus is especially precious?" he asked, with everyone agreeing enthusiastically. "Do you know the One who says 'Where two or three are gathered in my name, there am I in the midst'?" "Yes," the congregation responded. "Do we have two or three here tonight?" he asked as laughter resounded. People were packed in elbow to elbow. "Then is Jesus here?" Roberts then queried. "Yes," the congregation thundered. "Then you don't need me," said Roberts, who put on his hat and coat and departed. A man who had attended that meeting was asked what happened after that. He answered, "We all talked to Jesus and had a wonderful evening with Him."[2]

In America, revival continued apace. Atlantic City claimed only fifty unconverted adults in a population of sixty thousand. The first Baptist Church of Paducah added one thousand members in two months.

In Denver, the mayor declared a day of prayer, and by mid-morning all the churches were full, to the point that the stores had to close. The Colorado state legislature and the schools also closed for prayer. Some twelve thousand people jammed into theatres and public halls.

In Los Angeles, drunks and prostitutes seeking salvation filled the Grand Opera House. In Portland, Oregon, two hundred stores voluntarily closed for prayer for three hours at midday. Schenectady, New York, had a conversion column listing the names of those who had been converted the previous day.

Newspapers declared 1904 "The Year of the Holy Spirit," and featured headlines such as "Revival Shakes the Gates of Hell." The minutes of one Methodist church meeting reported that those gathered spontaneously broke into praise and singing.

Charismatic phenomena—tongues, ecstatic gifts, and so on—were in evidence, but the awakening was not sectarian nor centered around such developments. Indeed, all denominations were involved, and the revival even spawned entire new fellowships such as the Pentecostal and Holiness churches.

Not all meetings, however, were in the Pentecostal style. While some were attracted to emotional displays, others sought out quiet, orderly prayer and worship. Sometimes powerful preaching and teaching accompanied the revival, sometimes it did not. But there were some conditions that were true in all cases.

The worldwide revival of the late 1800s bore two distinct characteristics: the growth of Christianity and the improvement of society. True revival does not stop at the church door, but affects the entire society. In Wales, taverns went bankrupt and local police were unemployed because the crime rate dropped to practically zero. There was a slowdown in the mines caused not by workers but horses. They had learned to respond to cursing and swearing miners, and it took a while before they would respond to orders framed in more sanctified language and tone of voice.

In every area affected by the awakening there was a reduction of crime, drunkenness, gambling, and violence, and an increase of honesty, truthfulness, chastity—in short, morality in general. Another result was more responsible citizenship. These are the marks of an authentic movement of God.

Because of events such as those we have just outlined, the word *revival* signified a general spiritual awakening affecting masses of people across the entire spectrum of society and lasting a long time. In the new century, that definition would undergo some alteration.

CHAPTER SEVEN

The Valley of the Dry Bones

The Quenching of the Spirit

It should not surprise the informed Christian that a state of righteous living and spiritual fervor on the part of a nation is difficult to maintain even under the most favorable of circumstances. Like the Apostle Paul, Christians are aware of their own sinfulness and limitations. They are also aware, or should be, of attacks from without.

The countervailing forces to the Spirit-led revival were formidable, and soon mounted a vigorous insurgency. Liberal theology eroded popular acceptance of the Bible, challenging even the historicity of the death and resurrection of Jesus Christ. New gospels, such as Marxism, vied for attention. Man began to believe that he was master of his destiny and captain of his soul. Predictions of a golden age abounded.

Man's great faith in himself, however, received a shattering blow in World War I, which exposed the human potential for evil as few, if any, conflicts had done before. Where other wars had heightened spiritual interest, this one did not.

During the war period, churches drifted away from the primary prayer emphasis that had sustained each generation of Americans for almost two hundred years. Evangelists had previously relied on prayer and the power of the Holy Spirit. They now turned to other methods.

Showmanship Replaces Prayer Power

The years following 1915 could be called the days of the theatrical evangelists. Instead of dwelling on the love of God, preachers made excessive use of guilt. Furthermore, they directed the thrust of their ministry not so much to the soul or spirit as to the emotions. They substituted sensationalism for spirituality, and became known more for their financial irresponsibility and exaggerated conversion statistics than their godly living and preaching. (One evangelist, after a 1934 campaign on an Asian island, claimed three million converts—more than twice the population of the entire island.)

Two examples were Billy Sunday and Aimee Semple Macpherson, who live on in popular memory not so much because of their ministry, but because of their excesses. It may be of some significance that the song "Hooray for Hollywood" states that "everyone from Shirley Temple to Aimee Semple" is at home in the capital of show business. Clearly Miss Macpherson was considered one of the more interesting acts around, a sad commentary indeed. Evan Roberts and other revivalist leaders had tried to divert attention from themselves to God. The new breed of revivalists thrived on attention to themselves.

Among the results of sensational, show-business evangelism was a diminished respect for gospel preaching as a whole across the entire nation. Where the mainstream press had previously followed the awakening and treated it with respect, it now held an attitude of skepticism, with good reason. A diluted gospel and emotional approach produced shallow conversions often followed by backsliding. Thoughtful people began to suspect Christians of hypocrisy. Improvements in morality and responsible citizenship seldom accompanied these conversions. The term *revival* lost its vital currency and became roughly equivalent to a "rally," accompanied by much hoopla, promotion, etc., which stirs some excitement and draws some attention, but has no lasting effects.

Where in some quarters sensationalism prevailed, in the mainstream of American Protestantism the rule was deadness and formality. The sermon, not prayer, became the vehicle of persuasion. Prayer became a simple preliminary and pastoral office, rather than every believer's privilege and responsibility. Lengthy or memorized prayers replaced the spontaneous utterances of needy souls. Where prayers had previously been a stimulant, they now became a soporific.

The gospel of salvation through Jesus Christ was in many cases replaced by the "social gospel," a kind of quasi-Socialist New Deal with Scripture verses attached. This narrow creed downplayed or even denied the supernatural aspects of the Bible and set out to redeem society from racism and economic injustice rather than free the individual from sin. Although its intentions may have been honorable, by denying or downplaying the unique character of the gospel, it virtually guaranteed a decline in the Church's influence. In fact, that was precisely what happened. And without a vigorous Church, there is little hope for overcoming social evils of any sort.

Until this time, the longest period of religious decay in America had been about fifteen years. Every generation had seen visitations of God sweep the country, strengthening, restoring, and reclaiming the lost. But between 1915 and 1945, and entire generation grew up never knowing the effects of true revival.

An Exceptional Case

There was a measure of restoration from 1950-1960, sometimes called the Eisenhower Awakening. In Los Angeles in 1949, a ministers' fellowship at Pacific Palisades drew hundreds of pastors who responded with tears, confession, and fervent prayer. That August, the Student Briefing Conference brought a revival among Christian college students, which eventually swept across the nation and even became national news in 1950. Various converted screen actors formed The Hollywood Christian Group, which prayed together and worked with evangelist Billy Graham. Graham's three-week campaign in Los Angeles in 1950 broke all records and propelled him into a worldwide ministry which has continued unabated for nearly forty years. Graham is one of the few evangelists capable of commanding respect abroad. His life has been free from scandal and his ministry free from sensationalism.

While Graham concentrated on the gospel message of individual redemption from sin, others stressed physical healing, particularly those of a sensational, miraculous nature. While conversions often accompanied these healings, the increase in holy living so characteristic of true revival was often not present. During the Eisenhower Awakening there were jumps in church attendance and membership. However, unlike other seasons of revival, crime, alcohol abuse, violence, and immorality increased rather than decreased.

For their part, the 1960s and 1970s constitute the dark ages of American spiritual history. There was a blight of apostasy, represented by such trends as the "God is dead" movement. Cults sprang up, choking the faith like weeds. Religious nostrums from the East became popular, aided in their dissemination by rock groups such as the Beatles. The idea of objective truth fell into disfavor. Truth was redefined as what was true "for me." Everything became subjective in the "me generation." Whatever made one happy was held to be good. Slogans such as "better living through chemistry" baptized the use of dangerous drugs. The fallout from this disastrous period is still descending.

Some cite the Jesus Movement of the 1970s as a form of revival. It is true that there was a renewed interest in God and religion, particularly among young people of the counterculture. *Time* magazine even proclaimed 1976 the "Year of the Evangelical." However, the effect of the Jesus Movement on the nation as a whole was negligible. It was not a truly national movement but highly regional and did not affect all strata of society.

At present, the designation *born again* has become something of a byword, and it is often claimed that there are some fifty million born-again Christians in the United States. A broad variety of religious programs prevail on cable television, and a number of ministers have injected themselves into political and social issues with great zeal. While one cannot deny merit in much of this, it should be pointed out that crime, violence, and immorality are at an all-time high. One does not want to be utopian, but studies of the past support the conclusion that such a large number of Christians should have more of a redeeming influence on society at large.

Revival Abroad: A Reversal of Roles

Curiously, while Americans were turning away from God, people in other lands were turning to Him in great numbers. In the 1960s and 1970s revival fires blazed in such places as Britain, Central and South America, Southeast Asia, and Africa. Much of this has yet to be fully chronicled. One could argue that the Third World became the globe's spiritual center. One outstanding case is that of Korea.

That country had a long history of missionary work, but the spiritual leadership had gradually passed to the national brethren. In 1947, forty pastors gathered for prayer in North Korea. Each returned to his home church and called his congregation to a forty-day prayer meeting with services for prayer in mornings and evenings. Thousands attended, and during the revival which followed, over a thousand university students professed faith in Jesus Christ, at great cost to themselves and their families.

Communist leaders, famous for their hatred of Christianity, began to suppress the believers, imprisoning and even killing them. The churches immediately went underground, and many fled to South Korea. When North Korea invaded and occupied the South, they liquidated pastors en masse and turned churches into factories. However, as in many cases throughout church history, the believers thrived under persecution and revival grew in spite of the danger. After the invaders were expelled and a truce was signed in 1953, Christianity was to thrive in South Korea as it has in no other place in Asia and few places in the world.

Dr. Paul Yonggi Cho pastors one of the largest churches in the world, with a membership of untold thousands. Interestingly, Dr. Cho puts little stock in new methods that smack of marketing, but maintains the principles of revival from past awakenings. Though his church is huge, he cultivates small groups which meet in homes.[1] Dr. Cho's church now sends missionaries to America, a rather sad commentary on the spiritual condition of the United States and yet a note of hope that we may learn from the Korean prayer warriors.

Surveying the present situation, it is difficult to be optimistic. But the believer in Jesus Christ, who is indwelt by God's Holy Spirit, need never despair. God has revived us before, and can do so again. But there are some lessons we need to learn, or perhaps relearn, before any awakening can take place.

PART THREE

Stirring the
Embers

CHAPTER EIGHT

Characteristics of Revival

When most Americans think about revival, they picture a series of meetings lastings three days or longer with a visiting evangelist officiating. Often one church undertakes this effort, but for a big-name evangelistic campaign thousands of churches may plan together for years. (The "I Found It" campaigns would be one example, though the planning for these was relatively brief.) Preparations include extensive fund-raising and elaborate publicity. There may be youth nights, family nights, women's meetings, prayer breakfasts, and so on.

While much of this is necessary, none of these measures in themselves can bring revival. In the final analysis, only God can do that.

The Sovereignty of God

The study of past awakenings, whether in Biblical or American history, indicate that true revival cannot be planned. Revival is an act of God.

In Christian doctrine, the Holy Spirit is God, and, as the Scripture states, the Spirit moves "as *he* determines" (1 Corinthians 12:11, emphasis added), not how *we* determine. This is not to say that the Church is not involved. Though revival is the work of God, it always includes a vision for a movement of God on the part of individual Christians.

Evan Roberts, the inspiration behind the Welsh revival of 1904, brought a "message from God" to the churches. And the message had nothing to do with Roberts's personality or ministry. It had four simple steps: confession of sin, renunciation of bad habits, obedience to the Holy Spirit, and public confession of faith in Jesus Christ.

In a revived Church where many or all had taken these steps, evangelism might result as a matter of course. Once it starts, it seems to spring up spontaneously everywhere, requiring neither extensive fund-raising nor publicity campaigns.

The Biblical Pattern

Some of the characteristics of modern spiritual rallies have more to do with marketing tactics or mass psychology than the Scriptures and the Holy Spirit. Two characteristics of true revival may be found in the book of Acts: 1) Earnest prayer for the Holy Spirit's initiative; 2) home-centered ministry led by lay Christians.

The first and second chapters of Acts relate the outpouring of the Holy Spirit. At that time the believers met frequently for prayer, and Scripture indicates that the focus of the prayers was the coming of the Holy Spirit (Acts 1:8). The group numbered some 120 men and women (Acts 1:14, 15). Clearly there was no separation on the basis of sex. After the coming of the Holy Spirit in power, some three thousand were won to Christ (Acts 2:41). That is a ratio of one leader for twenty-five persons, and might be considered the beginning of the small-group concept. These three thousand met frequently in homes for table fellowship. And while Peter seemed to be the spokesman for the group, the movement did not depend on him; neither did it revolve around his personality. Teaching and prayer occurred all over town in all kinds of situations.

The Priority of Prayer

As strange as it may sound to some, in true revival prayer takes priority over preaching. One gets the impression that the Christians in the book of Acts were praying constantly. In the prayer revivals of the 1850s, it was as if people were saying, "We are hardened from instruction; it's time to pray."[1]

As the Holy Spirit begins to move, the wave of Christian vitality raises up preachers, evangelists, and teachers. But it's the prayer and the power that call the leaders, not the other way around. In a rally the evangelist seeks the sinner through persuasive preaching; in revival, the sinner seeks God.

The Works of the Spirit

When the Holy Spirit is present and moving in power, unusual phenomena may occur, just as they did in the book of Acts. Some Christians contend that these occurrences stopped after the apostolic age, which seems practically a denial of the character and sovereignty of God. We are told emphatically that God is sovereign, that He can do as He pleases. "Jesus Christ is the same yesterday and today and forever" (Hebrews 13:8).

Christians need to be open to the unusual and should not try to limit the Almighty to the kinds of action they happen to prefer. However, it must be stressed that past phenomena associated with revivals were works of *God*, not man. Christians should not try to *imitate* what has happened at other places in other times.

Though John Wesley was not known as a healer, healings

did take place through his ministry. Dreams and visions accompanied the revival of the late 1800s. Speaking in tongues was reported in India during the revival of 1903. On closer examination, none of these cases seems fraudulent, though spurious action is always possible, particularly with the gift of tongues, which is easily aped.

People who are drawn only by the unusual or miraculous tend to disappear when such happenings cease, as they always do. Some of those who gladly received healing from Jesus Christ were not nearly as receptive to His message of repentance and discipleship. In Scripture, miracles are not an everyday expectation, but occur at key junctures in Biblical history: the Exodus, the ministry of Christ, and so on.

Whatever miraculous or ecstatic phenomena accompany revival, such developments always take a subordinate place to simple but frequent meetings for prayer.

Results: Pervasive Influence

We are all familiar with the spectacle of the huge evangelistic rally with its enormous choir, thousands "going forward" at the culmination of the service (including some who are already Christians, who get up to encourage others), and jammed parking lots. So pervasive is this pattern that it is difficult to imagine a quiet movement of the Holy Spirit largely out of the media's eye, which spreads through lay-led prayer meetings, but which has a greater effect than the high-profile crusade with all its trappings. Yet it is those quiet movements of prayer that made America great.

Statistics are an uncertain currency on any subject, particularly in spiritual matters. Christians should be obedient, and not be enslaved by a "numbers mentality." However, it is safe to say that modern evangelistic rallies have not permeated the cities where they took place as did the prayer meetings in the past. As noted, Atlantic City a century ago reported only fifty unconverted adults in its entire population. Certainly nothing on that scale has recently happened. Neither has revival affected the entire nation, as it has before.

Respectability

An aura of wholesomeness pervades true revival. Those in positions of leadership realize that God is leading the people, even when unusual phenomena are present. But in the past, none of these unusual occurences have caused the revival, the Church, or the gospel to fall into disrepute.

As Arthur Strickland notes, it was when true principles of revival were discarded in favor of the sensational and the mechanical that the very word *revival* fell into disrepute.[2]

Of course, the media of today has a pronounced anti-Christian bias. Much reporting on religion is characterized by an astonishing ignorance of what the Christian faith teaches, along with an utter contempt for what it stands for. High-profile Christians are favorite bull's-eyes, sometimes with good reason.

However, one notes that religious people who maintain their dignity, who live the same in public and private, and who avoid financial scandal are generally treated fairly in the press. Mother Teresa and Billy Graham are two examples. Argentinian evangelist Luis Palau might be another. Those involved in revival must be able to say, like Jesus, "Which one of you accuses me of sin?"

Improved Society

The word *secular* does not appear in the Bible, and the Christian life is not to be bottled up in sealed compartments. God has always intended that good works should flow from faith and affect those in society at large. That is one true test of revival, which those of the past century, as noted, pass with flying colors. Nothing in recent years, and certainly nothing on the current scene, fits the bill. One hopes and prays that such efforts may come in the long term, in God's good time.

CHAPTER NINE

Guidelines for Prayer

A t this point I should stress that I have never lived through a time of true Spirit-borne revival. Neither, I would imagine, have most of my readers. Thus, I do not have endless personal experience to share on this point. I do believe, though, that genuine revivals of the past offer better guidelines than the experience of any individual. Certainly there is much room for flexibility, but some principles simply cannot be altered.

Desire

The first step would be a desire to pray. If you and your group have that, you are already on the right track. A spiritual hunger is a gift from God. However, it may require several sessions of prayer just to determine how God wants you to proceed. Pray about such issues as the time for prayer meetings, their frequency, whether children should be present, and so on. But don't become so cautious that you don't move ahead. You don't have to have all the answers before you proceed. The Holy Spirit can direct you the most easily as you set out in some direction, but remain open to His correction. Remember, you have the wind of the Spirit at your back. God is in charge, and He loves what you are doing for Him.

Everybody Prays

Scripture frequently notes that there is strength in numbers. As the proverb states, a threefold cord is not easily broken. One should approach prayer in concert with others. Perhaps copies of this or other books on prayer could be distributed to your pastor and interested staff at your church, such as the elders or youth leaders. Those in authority need to know that what you are doing fits within a larger context of prayer for revival. In addition, you need the support of their prayers.

The role assignments of mainstream society do not apply here. By centuries of faithfulness, women the world over have earned their reputation for being prayer warriors. And the youth and singles groups should not be overlooked. God is not a respecter of persons and has been known to move mightily among the young. Indeed, the young are often the most fervent and sincere in their prayers.

Moreover, prayer is something that *all* can do, the great unifier. In the various lists of spiritual gifts in the New Testament, one does not find prayer. Prayer is not so much part of the believer's ministerial function, but his priestly office. All believers in Jesus Christ are priests of God, with full access provided by Christ's sacrifice. It is axiomatic that such ones will be making full use of their office. No one may say of prayer, "It is not my gift."

There is another trap that must be avoided: the belief that those whose prayers were mightily answered in the past were a special, super-spiritual kind of people. This is simply not true. "The prayer of a righteous man is powerful and effective," says the Apostle James, writing to an ordinary group of Christians. "Elijah was a man just like us," the apostle adds. "He prayed earnestly that it would not rain, and it did not rain on the land for three and a half years. Again he prayed and the heavens gave rain, and the earth produced its crops" (James 5:16-18).

Opposition

Very early in your quest you should recognize that opposition will come. You have not merely chosen to indulge a harmless devotional exercise or quaint demonstration. On the contrary, you have become agents involved in a highly volatile and "offensive" activity.

Individually and collectively, prayer is a battle, part of the spiritual warfare between the Christian and the principalities and powers of the present age. The world is in the control of a usurper who has rejected the righful ruler. Christians are a spiritual insurgency—God's spies, as Malcolm Muggeridge puts it—and work for the true King. They do not fight alone.

The Apostle Paul urges Christians to equip themselves with "the full armor of God, so that you can take your stand against the Devil's schemes" (Ephesians 6:11). C. S. Lewis dealt with some of the Devil's tactics in his masterful *Screwtape Letters*, which, like practically everything Lewis wrote, is worthy of attention.

The Christian may be confident that the foe, though powerful and wily, has already been defeated. Christ's victory on the cross constituted D-Day for the enemy of souls. Christians are now a resistance force involved in mopping-up operations, awaiting the culmination of the ages, the arrival of the Kingdom of God.

All prayer ministry is challenging because it threatens

Satan more than anything else we do. Accordingly, Satan will throw all sorts of obstacles in your path. He will attempt to confuse you on the nature of prayer. He will encourage narrow and negative thinking. He will attempt to divide you. But through vigilance and God's power, he will be overcome.

Organization

Some Christians have acquired the rather strange notion that anything organized must be unspiritual. While there is no hard and fast pattern to prayer meetings, those which are unorganized to the point of disorder are contrary to Scripture. Paul insists that everything be done "in a fitting and orderly way" because God is not the author of confusion (1 Corinthians 14:40, 33).

People should know what you are doing; hence, some sort of pamphlet or flyer can be helpful. These simple statements were often used in the revivals of the past. Perhaps some information about past revivals may be included in them, as in the following example:

> Let's Raise a Concert of Prayer throughout the area of (wherever) for our country and the world. . . . In 1784, a tiny group of concerned Christians urged revival through prayer by means of a tract bearing this inscription: "A humble attempt to promote explicit agreement and visible union of God's people in extraordinary prayer for the revival of religion and the advancement of Christ's Kingdom." God's people responded, gathering regularly in churches, homes, workplaces, and public halls to pray for an outpouring of the Holy Spirit. The resulting awakening swept every state, town, and denomination in the United States. For fifty years, uninterrupted religious re-

newal and awakening blessed our country. Now, two hundred years later, God can do it again.

Place and time, of course, should be added. Once you are past the initial phase, word of mouth may take over. The news often spreads fast.

Keep the prayer meeting simple, bearing in mind that people's time is valuable. Accordingly, be considerate; set an exact starting and ending time, and be punctual. You might have an hour meeting if it is a breakfast or lunch period meeting, but many may prefer a more relaxed meeting of ninety minutes to two hours if it is a mid-morning coffee break or evening group.

One of Satan's tactics is to divert the focus of a meeting away from prayer. Accordingly, leaders should take the responsibility of guarding the format of the meeting and keeping it centered on prayer. It takes some skill to do this without being overbearing, but the task can be mastered. Theological disputes must be avoided by all means. As noted, the revivalists of old even put up signs forbidding such disputes. One must face the fact that on certain issues there will always be disagreement among well-meaning Christians.

As previously outlined, the prayer of the 1800s kept to a sixty-minute format, with only one hymn and one passage of Scripture allowed. In addition, only one prayer need at a time was permitted, and was then prayed for by one or two (or more) people before going on to the next need. Such a system is still ideal for a number of reasons.

For example, it minimizes interruptions and also allows the latecomer to make requests. Praying for each need in turn also allows for frequent breaks which minimize fatigue. Many people find it difficult to sit or stand for long periods of time with their eyes closed. Others find it hard to concentrate for lengthy stretches of time. And with this system, there is no need to write down or memorize a long list of requests. It also adds a sense of immediacy. The request is fresh on everyone's ears and hearts, and some brother or sister brings it to God right away, in a frame of mind to address it intelligently and compassionately.

If the meeting takes place at a mealtime, let those who need to eat continue to do so. Do not allow the presentation of prayer needs to become an autobiography; try to discourage people from talking about their problems in great detail because depressing details are distracting and can sap the group's energy. Move quickly to the solution—prayer.

At present, how many "prayer hours" are really fifteen minutes of singing, ten minutes of announcements, a twenty-minute Bible study, an eternity of gossip about absent members (often in the guise of enlightening our prayer), and five minutes of hurried prayer before everyone dashes off to choir practice? Is it any wonder such "prayer services" are poorly attended and generally ineffective?

Prayer is communication, not penance; it is a fundamentally human activity meant to be enjoyed, not endured. There is no need to affect a different kind of speech when addressing God, our Heavenly Father. Use a natural voice and the "you" form rather than the archaic "thees and thous" when praying. These are sometimes considered a more respectful form of prayer, but this idea is erroneous. In the time when it was used, "thou" was the *familiar* form of address, like the French and Spanish *tu,* always the preferred form for addressing God in those languages.

Some newcomers may be reluctant to pray out loud, and leaders should make full allowance of that fact. They should set an example that avoids stuffy or long prayers which often turn into sermons and which also discourage others from participating. Prayers should be spontaneous and fun. I believe that even laughter can be a form of prayer. And there are no Biblical stipulations about standing, sitting, or keeping one's eyes closed.

It may help the reluctant newcomer if the group stresses informal, one-sentence prayers, as outlined in Rosalind Rinker's book *Conversational Prayer.* This approach has many advantages. The one-sentence prayer is safe for new people, since almost anyone can think of one request or statement to say to God. Just as important, the format of brief prayers has the effect of limiting some of the more long-winded brethren, and thus keeping them from overwhelming others.

You could start your prayer time by saying, "What are you glad that God has done for you? Let's thank Him." Then give your example as a one-sentence prayer, such as "Thank you, God, for helping me be more patient today" or "Praise You, Jesus, for restoring my son to health," or whatever the item of praise might be. It is also helpful to have the group thank God for who and what He is.

Sometimes there is such an outpouring of requests—say, for the sick—that one-sentence intercessory prayer works very well. Names can be brought up in turn, with the rest of the group agreeing with the one praying. Praying in a circle and holding hands creates a sense of closeness and love for each other as we support these prayers lifted up for loved ones and friends.

The "fill in the blank" prayer—as in "God, _____ _____, will You help me?"—helps people to be both honest and spontaneous. In my experience, these short, sincere prayers go directly to God's heart.

Christians are transformed "by the renewing of your mind" (Romans 12:2), and the mind is not to be bypassed in prayer. Indeed, it should be actively engaged. Instead of just praying for Mary who has the flu, one should visualize Mary's condition. And as one prays for her, one could picture Mary revitalized, restored to health, and full of praise and the Holy Spirit.

My use of the word *visualization* may cause concern to some people, and hence a few words are in order. There has been much controversy about New Age prayer techniques, some of which are called visualization or "imaging." In these, it should be stressed, it is not God who is working, but the autonomous human mind. It is the *technique* which brings the result. In other cases, the process is linked to occultism. Obviously, that is not what I am discussing.

For the Christian, visualization does not bring about an answer to prayer; God does. The energy is not provided by the human mind, but by God's Holy Spirit. The visualization I am advancing is simply part of the mental processes resulting from the heartfelt *belief* that the all-powerful *God* is willing to answer the specific requests of His children, as He has outlined in His Word. Prayer should be done in the spirit of belief, with the full expectation that it will be answered. I believe Jesus prayed this way when He fed the five thousand. He looked up to Heaven, thanked the Father for the bread, broke the loaves, and gave the pieces to the disciples. He didn't ask the Father to do anything; He simply thanked Him for His provision. As the disciples continued distributing the loaves, God kept on supplying abundantly.

A visualization prayer for revival would be a good way to end meetings. With your group standing in a circle holding hands, you could begin like this:

"Father, we thank You for the joy of this time in Your presence. We thank You for sharing Your love with us through Jesus Christ. Our hearts are filled and renewed by your Holy Spirit.

"Each of us now lifts the person on our right to You, grateful for the work You are doing in that life. We praise You for Your wonder-working Spirit renewing the heart of our neighbor to the right." (Continue for the person on the left.)

"We sense the presence of Your Holy Spirit in our group and are filled with Him, whom we need to be part of our lives. We thank You for being here tonight and excitedly anticipate the great things You are doing."

Then continue in prayer, lavishly visualizing what would happen if God poured His healing love over *your* neighborhood, city, state, and nation.

CHAPTER TEN

Formats for Prayer

As the people of God have begun to come together to pray for revival in the San Francisco Bay Area, we have used several guidelines for meetings for prayer. These formats can be adapted for a personal and private prayertime of five minutes duration or expanded for use during a daylong (or longer) intercessory retreat. The three included here have been adapted from David Bryant's work with Concerts of Prayer,[1] from Larry Lea's prayer hour based on the Lord's Prayer,[2] and taken directly from the text of 2 Chronicles 7:14.

The Concert of Prayer

David Bryant's format for Concerts of Prayer teaches helpful principles of intercession. He divides the prayer period into two basic units: prayer for fullness, which he defines as revival and awakening within the Body of Christ; and fulfillment, or prayer for the expansion of Christ's Kingdom to the unsaved. And within those two main themes, prayer moves progressively from personal concerns to local concerns and broader categories—state, country, other nations, the world. The following is an overview of the Concert of Prayer format. The major sections are celebration, preparation, prayers for fullness, prayer for fulfillment, listening and testimony, and the grand finale—a time of commitment.

The celebration section focuses on God's holiness, transcendence, sovereignty and power, and His leadership. In a group setting, it could include praise in hymns and choruses, reports of God's answers to prayers offered up during previous Concerts, prayers of praise for God's faithfulness, for His Kingdom, for His Son. Carry this theme of celebration into personal devotions by coming to God in prayer, praising and acknowledging Him.

The preparation section provides focus through Scripture. In personal prayer, this could be quietly waiting on God to direct a spontaneous choice of verses, following an outline for Bible study, or choosing a book of the Bible to pray through systematically over a number of days or months. In a group prayer experience, a leader would introduce a portion of God's revelation.

The dedication section should be brief, silent, and very personal. It is a moment when the intercessor rededicates his life to Christ and should be part of every Christian's daily devotional time. It is a moment to reaffirm one's desire to serve the Church and the world through the ministry of intercession and to affirm to God a readiness to be used. Confess to God anything that may be hindering prayer, and receive His forgiveness, cleansing, and a fresh filling of His Spirit.

Add the following prayers if the dedication is for a group. Thank God for everyone gathered and ask God to blend the group so that it truly becomes a symphony of rejoicing, repentance, and intercession. Invite the Lord Jesus to take up His role as the High Priest of the meeting, bringing all together in His ministry. Ask Him to make the Concert His prayer meeting from beginning to end. Invite the Holy Spirit to guide and direct each person, blending hearts and voices in humility and love.

Praying for fullness or awakening in the Church should be included in private devotions as well as being an important component of corporate prayer. It would include prayers for local and global concerns as components in prayers of rejoicing, repentance, and request. For example, ask God for such a spirit of gratitude for all He has done already for us, personally and collectively, that all would delight to bring this joy to those who have never heard. Pray that Christians, in repentance and reconciliation, will band together to do the work of Christ. Ask God to fill His people with hearts of compassion for the earth's unreached. Include time to listen to what God has to say about His concerns for spiritual awakening, asking Him to show each person how to be an answer to these prayers.

The section on fulfillment (evangelization) among the nations is often overlooked in private devotions and corporate prayer because immediate personal needs and concerns seem so pressing. But intercessors need to include prayer for the unsaved in private and corporate prayer. Pray for Satan to be bound and fully routed. Praise God that Christ's victory on the cross breaks Satan's hold on nations and cultures. Ask God for awakening and spiritual hunger among the 2.5 billion people, such as Muslims, Chinese, Hindus, Buddhists, who have yet to hear of Christ. Pray that they may have a new sense of reality of God and an awakened desire to seek Him. Pray for the Christian Church within every country. Ask God to raise up a new missions thrust from every nation and people-group where communities of disciples already exist. Pray for America as a major sending base of missionary personnel. Pray that God would revive the Church in the U.S.A. so that the Christians here, representing nearly three-fourths of the world's evangelical resources and trained Christians, might release these God-given blessings for ministry to the earth's unreached. Pray that the revival will empower from on high the missionaries who go. Pray for world leaders and governments, and for the outcome of world events. Pray for leaders and governments that can encourage the free course of the gospel within a nation or within a people-group.

An important aspect of corporate or individual prayer is listening. Intercessors must cultivate a luxurious sense of waiting in the presence of God. What has God revealed in the area of the awakening of the Body of Christ? Has God given a new insight or vision, an exhortation, a word of repentance or hope? What has God said regarding the advancement of His Kingdom?

Bryant's grand finale concludes the Concert of Prayer. Each time Christians pray, God gives new revelation and insight either from His Word or His Spirit that brings a new level of understanding and requires a new commitment based on that revelation. The grand finale includes prayer for God's empowerment for ministry at a deeper level of responsibility. Action should always follow prayer.

The Lord's Prayer

The Lord's Prayer is a wonderful model for prayer, whether for personal devotions, small-group prayer, or a community-wide gathering of intercessors. It falls quite naturally into six sections. In personal devotions, one might spend only a minute or two focusing in prayer on each aspect. It's an ideal format for a small-group meeting for an hour or less. Participants can take turns informally leading each section. For example, a handful of intercessors who meet weekly at a major Bay Area corporation use the Lord's Prayer as the guide for lunch-hour prayer.

The Lord's Prayer gives common ground for gatherings that cross denominational lines and may include Roman Catholic and Protestant believers, such as one might find in a corporate gathering.

Sections with brief guidelines for praying through each one follow. For more detail see Larry Lea's *Could You Not Tarry One Hour?* When praying through each section, expand the prayers to include local and global concerns in prayers of praise and repentance as well as requests. Focus on prayers for revival of the Body of Christ and prayers for evangelism of the unsaved.

During the first section, "Our Father which art in heaven, hallowed is thy name," focus on His divinity, sovereignty, power, holiness, and love. Call Him by His names and acknowledge His greatness. He is our Father, Shepherd, King, El-Shaddai (The All-sufficient One), Jehovah-Jireh (God Is Provider), Jehovah-Shalom (God Is Peace), Healer, Righteous Judge, Our Banner. Respond to His greatness, listen for His voice. A text from the Psalms collects the concepts of this exalted prayer: "Come, let us bow down in worship, let us kneel before the Lord our Maker; for he is our God and we are the people of his pasture, the flock under his care" (Psalm 95:6, 7).

The second section, "Thy kingdom come, thy will be done," begins by praying for His reign and rule in and through one's own life. Then pray this prayer for immediate family members. Expand this vision of God's reign and rule to include the local church, community, state, nation, and finally the entire world.

Nearly everyone has many personal concerns and needs that readily come to mind in the third section, "Give us this day our daily bread." Examine each concern and ask, "What if that prayer included every person on earth, what would the prayer be?" Take, for example, wanting health and good things—education, housing, jobs, mates—for our children. Expand that prayer to the furthest limit, and it becomes a prayer that all the children of the world would have a chance to grow up healthy—mentally, physically, and spiritually. Then ask God how He might use this prayer group to answer that prayer. Many ministries to those in need have been birthed in just such a prayer. Is God calling you to be an answer to the "daily bread" prayer of others less fortunate?

However we word the forgiveness section, the message is the same. God commands His children to forgive the faults of others and promises to forgive our shortcomings as we forgive from the heart. Sometimes unforgiveness is painfully easy to identify. Other times the Holy Spirit must be invited to reveal areas of our lives that need cleansing. David realized the importance of maintaining transparency in prayer: "Search me, O God, and know my heart; test me and know my thoughts. See if there is any offensive way in me, and lead me in the way everlasting" (Psalm 139:23). Ask God to forgive you. Forgive and release others. If you can't truly forgive from your heart, will to forgive those who have sinned against you.

The fifth section, "Lead us not into temptation, but deliver us from evil," is a prayer for strength to resist worldly temptations. Put on the whole armor of God as outlined in Ephesians 6:13-18.

The last section, "For thine is the kingdom and the power and the glory forever," is a time of commitment in and to Christ in celebration of who He is. The victory that is ours in Him needs to be declared each time we pray. Pray through Philippians 4:4-7. Sing Isaiah 51:11 to the Lord: "The ransomed of the Lord will return. They will enter Zion with singing; everlasting joy will crown their heads. Gladness and joy will overtake them, and sorrow and sighing will flee away."

2 Chronicles 7:14

2 Chronicles 7:14, a familiar Scripture to intercessors, declares a convenant between the Lord and His people. Christians today long for this covenant to be realized in our day and our country before it is too late. "If my people, who are called by my name, will humble themselves and pray and seek my face and turn from their wicked ways, then will I hear from heaven and will forgive their sin and will heal their land." This text makes a powerful format for an intercessory prayer meeting, whether it is a gathering of two or three in His name or hundreds from the community of faith.

"If my people who are called by my name will humble themselves . . ." Pray that Christians would more deeply recognize the sovereignty of God in their lives. Intercede for a renewed, lively dependence on God and an end to "Christian atheism" among the churched. Ask God to melt down the barriers of pride that separate, isolate, and weaken the Body of Christ—whether those barriers are due to race, gender, age, class, or to aspects of theology and worship that are nonessentials to salvation. In Jesus' name, call to repentance those who, while calling themselves Christian, are not church members and who seem to worship material goods and success more than surrendering to a responsible servant lifestyle. In Jesus' name, call those who have abandoned their Christian teaching and sought enlightenment in the New Age cults and the occult with their emphasis on the divinity of man, power, and inflated pride. Pray for a renewed sense of godliness throughout America, the country with "In God we trust" on its coins.

"If my people, who are called by my name will pray. . . ." Quietly ask God to open hearts to Himself for fellowship with Him that is rich and sweet. Pray for a listening heart within each person to easily hear all that He has to communicate. Pray that the Holy Spirit will convict pastors in the area of disciplined prayer and that they will make time alone with the Lord the Number One priority of their busy schedules. Ask God to give pastors one hour a day with Him. Never has there been a true revival that was not begun in prayer. Ask God to raise up an overwhelming renewed desire for prayer among His people. Our country was founded in an attitude of prayer and dependence on God on the part of the leaders. Pray that a holy fear of God leads to a profound reliance on prayer in our nation's legislature. Pray for Christians in countries throughout the world, for an outcry of prayers lifted to God on behalf of every nation.

"If my people, who are called by my name will seek my face. . . ." After each person shares an area of his or her life that is a prayer need, pray that the person will seek God's will in that situation, completely offering the outcome to Him. Ask God by His Spirit to help each one to hear and obey. Pray for greater willingness to be transformed by the renewing of our minds, wills, and hearts into a people God can trust and use. Pray for the authority of God's Word, that it once again will be regarded as the standard against which all else is judged. Pray that respect for the Bible will be restored in homes, schools, government, and business and unto the ends of the earth. Pray that Christian ethics and morality will once again become normative in all areas of society. Pray for an end to relativism and do-your-own-thing amorality.

"If my people, who are called by my name will turn from their wicked ways. . . ." Pray that the Church as a whole will be delivered from wicked ways—immorality among church leaders, liberal views that sanction sexual sin, prejudice, insensitivity to the real needs of people, a holier-than-thou attitude, lip-service religiosity, and apathy toward true spirituality. Pray that America will turn from national wickedness—permissiveness toward abortion, homosexuality, New Age religious teaching, overspending, corruption in government, etc.

"Then will I hear from heaven and will forgive their sin and will heal their land." Enter a time of intercession for the Body of Christ, our country, and the world. Use Daniel's prayer for the nation Israel as inspiration (Daniel 9:4-19). Ask God to hear the prayers of Christians throughout the world who cry out for a new wave of revival. Pray for an outpouring of God's blessing worldwide. Ask God to forgive corporate sin in the Body of Christ in its multiple forms and that these sins be completely blotted out by His mercy. Ask for a spirit of forgiveness within the Church so that as revival begins and many people return to holiness they will find welcome, not resentment and bitterness, in the church family. Pray one-sentence intercessory prayers for healing for every aspect of the land.

Fall completely silent for a moment and listen to God. What has God said during the prayer-time? God is calling each person to be an answer to these prayers. Pray for each person's commitment and place of service. End the time of prayer with celebration, and praise God for the victory He has provided in Christ.

CHAPTER ELEVEN

The Challenge

The End of the Ages?

In recent decades, people have begun to seriously wonder about the future of the human race. The degree of concern might be indicated by the success of a book called *The Late Great Planet Earth,* which made its author, Hal Lindsey, the best-selling Christian author of the 1970s. Only a populace unsure of where it is headed could contribute to that situation. And little has changed in the ensuing years, in spite of the general optimism of the Reagan years.

Every day the media assails Americans with news of crime, violence, famines, wars, pollution, earthquakes, and, of course, the possibility of a nuclear holocaust. People wonder if there will be a safe or habitable world for them and their children. In the face of the current AIDS epidemic, perhaps some recall the predictions of scientists that all diseases would soon be eradicated. Confronted with Three Mile Island and Chernobyl, others doubtless recall promises of boundless energy forever, without possibility of the slightest mishap. These broken promises and failed predictions have created a nation of skeptics and cynics.

This sense of impending doom may have contributed to

the generally amoral climate in which we live. Alcoholism, drug abuse, infidelity, weakened parental authority, civic corruption: all these have contributed to the present quagmire in which we find ourselves. We have contributed to it. We have made a mess of things. We have sinned.

America: Then and Now

As a result, Americans are not what they once were and our nation is not what it once was. Though not chosen in the sense of Israel, it was nevertheless a light to the nations and an inspiration to those all across the world who aspired to freedom. In the past, America earned the admiration and respect from its deadliest enemies. Even Adolf Hitler wrote of "the unheard of internal strength of this state," referring to America, in *Mein Kampf*. But this has now changed.

The charges from people such as the Ayatollah Khomeini or Daniel Ortega that America is a decadent society cannot always be written off as political propaganda. They are quite often true. The peoples of the world are bemused by America's moral confusion and weakness. They wonder why Americans divorce so readily and why American children who have everything waste themselves in drug abuse. Nations, like individuals, are living letters, known and read by others. America's current testimony, while far from extinguished, has certainly dimmed.

Before the revivals of the 1800s there was much skepticism, with ideologists such as Voltaire claiming that Christianity was destined to pass away in a matter of years. In spite of recent attempts at reform, we still face the specter of atheistic Marxism-Leninism, a militant materialist creed which posits an end to religious belief, and which has viciously persecuted and killed our Christian brothers and sisters for seventy years.

In short, many are the Goliaths who taunt us, asking who

112

we will send forth. But what will we do about this state of affairs?

Turning to God: The Path of Revival

Is it not time to turn again to the God of our fathers? Is it not time to call on Him to begin another mighty movement of prayer? Is it not time to call upon God to help reestablish this great nation with God as her true Sovereign and Lord? We have the promise in His Word, which bears repeating:

> If my people, who are called by my name, will humble themselves and pray and seek my face and turn from their wicked ways, then will I hear from heaven and will forgive their sin and will heal their land. (2 Chronicles 7:14)

This is one of the more self-explanatory texts in all of the Bible. It is also one which has been proven, as the prophet Jeremiah notes:

> "When seventy years, are completed for Babylon, I will come to you and fulfill my gracious promise to bring you back to this place. For I know the plans I have for you," declares the Lord, "plans to prosper you and not to harm you, plans to give you hope and a future. Then you will call upon me and come and pray to me, and I will listen to you. You will seek me and find me when you seek me with all your heart. I will be found by you." (Jeremiah 29:10-13)

For the reader who has not yet placed his or her faith in the Son of God, I offer this prayer as a pattern:

O God, make me a person of faith. Jesus, I ask You into my life and accept You as Lord over me. Forgive me for my sins and for my lack of faith, and restore my spirit to believe. Holy Spirit, teach me and open my heart so that I might dare to place my hope in things that are yet unseen. Help me yield to Your standards of righteousness and love. I want to be strong in tough times with faith that never wavers and a trust that rebuilds.

It is impossible to deny that there is a deep hunger for God in the land, and even around the world. Why else would cults and quackish New Age teachings be able to flourish? The barren secularism of our times has left the soul of America parched, ready for the waves of a prayer and Spirit-led revival to sweep over it. People are waiting for someone to guide them into the truth, and that is the task of the Church.

For those who belong to Jesus Christ, we should confess that we have failed in that task. Part of the reason is that our idea of revival has been backwards. We have depended on great men to carry the day, instead of God Himself. We have trusted in the techniques of marketing and publicity instead of the power of the Holy Spirit. We have asked God to bless our pet ideas and schemes instead of submitting ourselves humbly to His will.

We should cry out to the Father to revive us again, as He has so many times before. Like Hannah, we need to enter into a dynamic partnership with God, realizing that the prayer of one person counts for much—especially prayer accompanied by faith. And faith, as Hudson Taylor noted, both attempts great things *for* God, and expects great things *from* God. The gloom, complacency, and negativity characteristic of the Church needs to be replaced with *hope,* as the New Testament explains in a prayer of the Apostle Paul:

May the God of hope fill you with all joy and peace as you trust in him, so that you may overflow with hope by the power of the Holy Spirit. (Romans 15:13)

Picturing Revival

I live in the San Francisco Bay area, and find it exciting to visualize revival sweeping California. Of course, any city can be substituted; the important thing is that all have a clear picture of hope in the Lord.

But imagine what would happen if a city like San Francisco turned to God. Picture noontime prayer meetings in the financial district, packed with Christians and seekers after God. Picture waves of awakening spreading in to Nob Hill, North Beach, Pacific Heights, and the Marina. Picture renewal in the avenues, with skid-row residents healed of alcoholism and drug addiction. In Christ, they find worth and release from their bondage to self-loathing. True social reform would sweep San Francisco. Churches would be filled with families from all over the world, worshiping, praising, and praying. Imagine picking up the *San Francisco Chronicle* and reading:

BAY AREA PRAYER REVIVAL BRINGS AWAKENING TO SAN FRANCISCO

Imagine the story being picked up by national media, and touching off a flurry of letters and telephone calls. Picture the revival moving to other cities, where Christians would proclaim that if God could so mightily visit San Francisco, He will also come to them if they pray. See the awakening spreading to the nation as a whole, and onward to other countries in the world, bringing with it a spirit of generosity and even a relaxation of international tensions. Or perhaps one could visualize a revival starting in some other country such as Canada or Mexico and spreading to the United States.

This all may seem unrealistic—a fairy tale, even—to some readers, but there is no good reason why it should be. Christians do not have faith in faith, nor even faith in prayer. Remember the One who is the *object* of prayer: the God revealed in the Hebrew-Christian Scriptures. He is not one to be put in a box. He is the omnipotent, omniscient Creator of Heaven and earth, and nothing is impossible to Him. He is the potter, we are the clay. And He is not the aloof, detached Deity portrayed in Deism. He is both transcendent and immanent. Many times in the past He has performed His works in full view of everyone. And some of the greatest movements have come in our own country. To deny that revival can come again practically amounts to a denial of the character of God. That the culmination of the ages—whose timing is known only to God—may be approaching is only a further incentive to seek God's face.

As the Apostle Paul wrote, "But thanks be to God! He gives us the victory through our Lord Jesus Christ" (1 Corinthians 15:57). The grace of our Lord Jesus Christ be with you. Amen.

Bibliography

Beardsley, Frank Grenville. *A History of American Revivals*. Boston: American Tract Society, 1904.

Bryant, David. *With Concerts of Prayer*. Ventura, CA: Regal Books, 1985.

Candler, Warren H. *Great Revivals and the Great Republic*. Nashville: Publishing House of the M. E. Church, 1924.

Cho, Paul Y. and Hostetler, Harold. *Successful Home Cell Groups*. Plainfield: Logos International, 1981.

Edwards, Jonathan. *Some Thoughts Concerning the Present Revival of Religion in New England*, 1742.

———. *Edwards on Revivals*. New York: Dunning and Spalding, 1832.

Finney, Charles G. *Memoirs of Rev. Charles G. Finney*. New York: Revell, 1876.

Goen, C. C. *Works of Jonathan Edwards*, Vol. 4: *The Great Awakening*.

Hale, E. M., editor. *Life and Letters of Benjamin Franklin*. Eau Claire, WI: E. M. Hale and Company.

Lacy, Benjamin R., Jr. *Revivals in the Midst of the Years*. Richmond: John Knox Press, 1943.

Labaree, Leonard W., editor. *The Autobiography of Benjamin Franklin*. New Haven, CT: Yale University Press, 1964.

Lea, Larry. *Could You Not Tarry One Hour?* Altamonte Springs, FL: Creation House, 1987.

Lovejoy, David S. *Religious Enthusiasm and the Great Awakening*. Englewood Cliffs, NJ: Prentice-Hall, 1969.

Muncy, W. L., Jr. *A History of Evangelism in the United States*. Kansas City: Central Seminary Press, 1945.

National Conference on Prayer for Spiritual Awakening. Cassette tapes, Numbers 4, 11, 16. Ridgecrest Baptist Conference Center, 1981.

Orr, J. Edwin. *The Second Evangelical Awakening in America*. London: Marshall, Morgan and Scott, 1952.

———. *The Fervent Prayer*. Chicago: Moody Press, 1974.

———. *The Eager Feet.* Chicago: Moody Press, 1975.

Prime, S. I. *The Power of Prayer.* New York, 1859.

Rinker, Rosalind. *Conversational Prayer.* Waco: Word Books, 1970.

Sweet, William Warren. *Revivalism in America.* New York: Charles Scribner's Sons, 1945.

Strickland, Arthur B. *The Great American Revival.* Cincinnati: Standard Press, 1934.

Zundel, Veronica, editor. *Famous Prayers.* Grand Rapids: Eerdmans, 1983.

Notes

INTRODUCTION

1. Frank Grenville Beardsley, *A History of American Revivals* (Boston: American Tract Society, 1904), p. 309.

CHAPTER FOUR Religious Roots

1. See Paul C. Vitz, *Censorship: Evidence of Bias in our Children's Textbooks* (Ann Arbor, MI: Servant Books, 1986).
2. Jonathan Edwards, *Some Thoughts Concerning the Present Revival of Religion in New England*, 1742.
3. See W. L. Muncy, Jr., *A History of Evangelism in the United States* (Kansas City: Central Seminary Press, 1945), p. 40.
4. Quoted in David S. Lovejoy, *Religious Enthusiasm and the Great Awakening* (Englewood Cliffs, NJ: Prentice-Hall, 1969), p. 83.
5. *The Autobiography of Benjamin Franklin*, Leonard Labaree, ed. (New Haven, CT: Yale University Press, 1964), p. 175.
6. Quoted in Warren H. Chandler, *Great Revivals and the Great Republic* (Nashville: Publishing House of the Methodist Episcopal Church, 1924).
7. See Roger Lundin and Mark Noll, *Voices from the Heart: Four Centuries of American Piety* (Grand Rapids, MI: Eerdmans, 1987).
8. William Warren Sweet, *Revivalism in America* (New York: Charles Scribner's Sons, 1945), p. 41.
9. Muncy, *A Histroy of Evangelism in the United States,* p. 52.
10. Sweet, *Revivalism in America*, p. 22.
11. Quoted in *Life and Letters of Benjamin Franklin*, E. M. Hale, ed. (Eau Claire, WI: E. M. Hale and Company), p. 328.
12. Benjamin R. Lacy, *Revivals in the Midst of the Years* (Richmond, VA: John Knox Press, 1943), p. 62.

CHAPTER FIVE The Prayer Century

1. S. I. Prime, *The Power of Prayer* (New York: n.p., 1859), p. 29.
2. Lacy, *Revivals in the Midst of the Years*, p. 65.
3. Quoted in Arthur B. Strickland, *The Great American Revival* (Cincinnati: Standard Press, 1934), p. 44.
4. Edwin J. Orr, *The Eager Feet* (Chicago: Moody Press, 1975), p. 52.
5. *Ibid.*, p. 54.
6. *Ibid.*, p. 56.
7. *Ibid.*, p. 63.
8. Lacy, *Revivals in the Midst of the Years*, p. 105.
9. Edwin J. Orr, *The Second Evangelical Awakening in America* (London: Marshall, Morgan and Scott, 1952), p. 25.
10. Beardsley, *A History of American Revivals*, p. 233.
11. Orr, *The Second Evangelical Awakening in America*, p. 33.
12. Lacy, *Revivals in the Midst of the Years*, p. 112.
13. Orr, *The Second Evangelical Awakening in America*, p. 33.
14. *Ibid.*, p. 39.
15. Beardsley, *A History of American Revivals*, p. 227.
16. Orr, *The Second Evangelical Awakening in America*, p. 61.
17. *Ibid.*, p. 58.
18. Lacy, *Revivals in the Midst of the Years*, p. 113.
19. Charles Finney, *Memoirs of Rev. Charles G. Finney* (New York: Revell, 1876), p. 444.
20. Prime, *The Power of Prayer*. p. 29.
21. Edwin Orr, in *National Conference on Prayer for Spiritual Awakening*, Ridgecrest Baptist Conference Center, 1981, Tapes 4, 11, 16.
22. Muncy, *A History of Evangelism in the United States*, p. 144.
23. Beardsley, *A History of American Revivals*, p. 246.
24. Lacy, *Revivals in the Midst of the Years*, p. 121.
25. Quoted in Veronica Zundel, *Famous Prayers* (Grand Rapids, MI: Eerdmans, 1983), p. 73.
26. Cited in Lundin and Noll, *Voices From the Heart*, pp. 172, 173.

CHAPTER SIX Onward to the Year of the Holy Spirit

1. Cited in Lundin and Noll, *Voices from the Heart*, p. 235.
2. Orr, *National Conference on Prayer*.

CHAPTER SEVEN The Valley of the Dry Bones

1. See Paul Y. Cho and Harold Hostetler, *Successful Home Cell Groups* (Plainfield, NJ: Logos International, 1981).

CHAPTER EIGHT Characteristics for Revival

1. Orr, *The Second Evangelical Awakening in America,* p. 130.
2. Strickland, *The Great American Revival,* p. 17.

CHAPTER TEN Formats for Prayer

1. David Bryant, *With Concerts of Prayer* (Ventura, CA: Regal Books, 1985).
2. Larry Lea, *Could You Not Tarry One Hour?* (Altamonte Springs, FL: Creation House, 1987).